More praise for

ASHES
to
ADMIN

'What happens when we die alone or without money?
If we're lucky, council funeral officer Evie King steps in.
Evie offers a fascinating and often amusing insight into an
aspect of death that is universally feared. A surprisingly
uplifting meditation on what death has to teach us about life'

Georgie Vestey, Dead Honest Podcast

'A fascinating, poignant and funny insight into the slightly
macabre world of a council funeral officer'

Diane Morgan

'I was gripped from the first moment I started reading'

Joe Wilkinson

For the soul I hold an umbrella for.

ASHES
to
ADMIN

EVIE KING

MIRROR BOOKS

m
B

MIRROR BOOKS

All of the events in this story are true,
but names and details have been changed to protect
the identities of individuals.

© Evie King

1

Published in Great Britain and Ireland in 2023 by
Mirror Books, a Reach PLC business.

www.mirrorbooks.co.uk
@TheMirrorBooks

Print ISBN 9781915306302
eBook ISBN 9781915306319

Cover illustration by David Rigby
Chapter illustrations by Adam Ward

Printed and bound in Great Britain by
CPI Group (UK) Ltd, Croydon, CR0 4YY

CONTENTS

Acknowledgements

Mum, Dad, Nick, Lee and James for being my family
and the people who shaped me.

Rich, Stew and Bruce for the support you never knew you
were giving a weird kid, but which meant so much.

Catie and Jane for real friendship.

Cathy for giving me the chance to be who
I always was, Steve for guiding me through,
and Chris and Ruth for morale and snacks.

Jodie, Lisa, Rhia and Martin for making
everything go hitch-free.

Jason, Jo, Angus
and Mirror Books for backing me.

Mair for first taking an interest in my story.
Dave for illustrating it beautifully.

And last but not least, my people whose lives and deaths
have touched mine and made all this possible.

Evie

Prelude

I went back to her grave six months after the funeral. More than a year since her body had been found. I still didn't know her name.

I was there to watch the laying of her gravestone. One of the many odd facts I have learned in this job is that you can't lay a stone right away. The ground is still settling for many months. Lay it too early and it will just end up getting swallowed by the earth. Go forth with that useless information and do with it as you will.

The stone was dedicated to 'the unknown lady'. Seeing those words permanently etched was a gloomy visual metaphor. An admission of defeat. Her true identity would never be known. Along with how she died. Though I had my own personal theories. Unprovable, but borne out by clues later left at the graveside and contact from medics who had attended similar scenes. Along with warnings to back away.

I chatted to her for a bit. Acknowledging at one point that I knew full well I was talking to nobody, believing as I do in nothing much. I apologised for leaving her there unclaimed, said I had done my best, better even, if I did say so myself.

I discussed my theory with her. Listened to the wind to see if an answer came back on it, and then quickly remembered that, oh yeah, I don't believe in that stuff.

I told her I had met her in fever dreams I'd had during a virus. We were up on the cliff edge on a stormy night, even though the weather would have been fine at the time of year she died, nice bit of pathetic fallacy from my subconscious there. I asked her what had happened, what was about to happen. She fixed me with a stare and said nothing. When I woke up, it felt like she was still there. I had to get out of bed and walk around to return myself to reality. It was a bad virus, to be fair, but I had perhaps thrown myself into this case slightly too much, even on a good day. That's the nature of the job though, if you do it properly.

So what line of work could possibly lead someone to this peculiar situation? And how did I end up at the graveside of an unclaimed body, having a chat with the wind and the soil on my day off from it? To answer that, we'll have to leave this place, and go back to the beginning.

Introduction

'Whatever became of the moment when one first knew about death?' asked Tom Stoppard's Rosencrantz. 'There must have been one. A moment. In childhood. When it first occurred to you that you don't go on forever. Must have been shattering, stamped into one's memory. And yet, I can't remember it.'

Can you? It seemed to just seep in, right? Nobody delivered the news directly, there was no memo, you didn't get the talk, it arrived by osmosis, through overheard conversations and fairy stories. Was gently reinforced every time someone got flattened in a cartoon or fell into hot lava in a video game. Then unhelpfully retracted when the cartoon character popped back into three-dimensional life, and the video game hero regenerated as good as new, on account of your having ten lives left.

But we still saw it as a death when it happened and knew full well, thanks to a trail of dead pets and grandparents, that we ourselves only had one life left. And the worst part is, we were made to quietly and internally assimilate this fairly devastating knowledge against a real world backdrop of 'we don't talk about that'. Made to feel anxious and alone in something that is the single biggest unifying factor of them all. But we will be talking about it, a lot, over the next two-hundred-odd pages, so let's start off with the basics.

You're going to die.

That's not meant as a threat, by the way. Just establishing a premise. It's an obvious fact but oft forgotten. Wilfully, of course. As though you could ever really forget. But death is fairly absent from everyday life. Kept at bay with a deft society-wide cognitive dissonance that allows us to both know this visceral information and yet somehow concurrently not know it. What is first consumed and filtered through the unreality of television, films and games ends up being something that can't happen in reality either. Even death in the actual news seems irrelevant to us, something that happens elsewhere, to someone else, in murder scenes, hospitals and war zones, not to us in our freshly hoovered, semi-detached house, perish the thought.

We imagine that we can somehow invoke it by signing up for a funeral plan or writing a will. Best to ignore it and hope it bypasses us, like a squirrel that believes by staying perfectly still it becomes invisible. We decide that it can't happen if we don't think about it. Something that made the Coronavirus pandemic, that I am writing in the midst of, all the more traumatic, because not thinking about it was made temporarily much more difficult. Though all of the WhatsApped memes, Zooming, baking and crafting seemed to go some way towards maintaining our bubbles as the death stats were announced in abstract at 2pm each day. But more of that later.

I have always been struck by people referring to any death as unexpected. I realise that in such cases they are specifically referring to a sudden, rather than a clearly signposted demise, but you can die the same day you are born so it's permanently on the table. I myself should already be long dead, gone before I even knew I was alive, and the scar from my bodged emergency surgery at a few weeks old, along with the occasional twinge, either phantom pain or from scar tissue, gives me a permanent humbling reminder that I shouldn't exist and one day won't again; death is more than expected, it is guaranteed. Should our brains slip up momentarily, say when passing a graveyard or funeral home, and remind us of this, our ultimate fate, we rally, assure ourselves that it won't be for a very long time. We dye our hair to fool ourselves into believing this time is even further away than it is, a time which is so far removed from the moment we are inhabiting right now that it bears no relevance. But one day, the here and now will meet the long way off, and they will become one and the same moment. What will that moment look like?

On the very rare occasion that we contemplate this, we tend to dream of an idealised made-for-tv-movie departure. Soft focus, surrounded at our bedside by doting loved ones, our brow being mopped, we gesture for people to come in closer, whisper some wise and loving last words, whilst somehow having fabulous hair, before exhaling deeply as our head droops gracefully to one side, our final repose. A hand sweeps across our face as our eyelids are gently closed for us. And, scene.

The funeral that follows is an outpouring of affection and grief. Eulogies, anecdotes, songs and poems tell our story. The attendees, their tears, the flowers, all of these things stack up to validate our life; prove we mattered. The people left behind will carry the memory of us with them, and we won't be forgotten, well not for a while anyway.

Not everyone gets this ending of course. There are many categories of person who have nobody around, willing or able to give them a funeral. Those who lived to a ripe old age and whose loved ones had all pre-deceased them. Those who became estranged from their families somewhere along the way and never made amends. Those who lived deliberately solitary lives, not caring for company. Those who became outcasts due to criminal or deviant behaviour. Those whose bodies went unclaimed and who remain anonymous.

In the absence of anyone willing or able, somebody has to arrange and attend their funerals, and that person is me, or someone like me: a local authority staff member charged with carrying out Section 46 funerals under the Public Health Act. It sounds pretty cold when you put it like that – the stark disposal of unclaimed remains so as to prevent a public health hazard – and to be blunt, in some corners it can be, but I have tried to use my position to elevate it beyond a task and to create genuine funerals that seek to rediscover the individual one last time; because if a job's worth doing, it's worth doing properly. Only trouble is, if a job is to do with people's lives, doing it properly can become existential and all-consuming. And on that spoiler, I would like to invite you to look back with me at my first few years in this, the most interesting, arduous, existentially exhausting, and rewarding job I ever did.

Not that there's much competition for that title. I mean, I once worked as a mobile receptionist for a company with an enforced hairdo and makeup policy and an annual best groomed lady award; like Crufts, but for human women. During one assignment, an MP made me carry a well-used Sainsbury's bag full of Viagra up the stairs for him. The only way was up from there. Anyway, I would like to give you a tour of my caseload – or 'my people' as I affectionately call them – and tell their stories one more time, along with the impact they have had on my own, both in helping me to find a vocation after many years of jobs I hated, and in connecting me, ironically through having one foot permanently in death, more deeply with life. Because what is the value of life without death? To quote Stoppard one more time: 'Eternity is a terrible thought. I mean, where's it going to end?'

But before we get into all that, let's get the business end of things out of the way and start at the very technical start: the process itself. If I whip you through it now, it'll save time later. So, when a person dies in these circumstances, I get a call, typically from a care home or a coroner, less typically from a relative, although this is on the increase both within my own caseload and across the country, so allow me to instantly digress. (And just when we were starting to drill down too – sorry, messy nature of the job.)

Not everyone who has their funeral carried out under

Section 46 is alone or estranged. There will also be individuals with next of kin to mourn them, but who are unable to bear the costs of the arrangements due to financial hardship and the rising price of funerals. The average funeral currently stands at around £4,000, which most people, including me, don't have lying around. There is a Department for Work and Pensions contribution for those on benefits, however this can only be claimed if your entire family is receiving state assistance, and that includes adoptive and step-relations, as well as long-lost cousin Sven from Siberia who nobody ever met.

Those who somehow manage to jump that particular hurdle will then be dismayed to learn that the DWP contribution is, at the time of writing, registration, fees for burial or cremation, plus £1,000 for costs. This sounds a lot, but costs include funeral director, coffin, headstone, flowers, all of which stretch well beyond the £1,000. And that's not me being all opinionated and critical, the DWP site itself states that it will not cover the entire cost of a funeral. Incredibly, this contribution is actually the new and improved amount, having just risen from a paltry £700 for the first time since 2003. It is to be welcomed of course, but when you consider the many years of inflation, it's not really a rise, it's just the same difference. The same gaping distance that cannot be bridged considering how the industry has increased their costs by many times the rate of inflation during that period.

I have taken several phone calls from people who were unwell and in poverty, worried that their spouse or children would be unable to afford their imminent deaths and making enquiries about a Section 46 funeral for themselves. Talking someone through the process whilst they are still breathing, telling them where their family should send their body, it's some of the most messed-up and difficult work I have had to do.

Bereaved families come to councils as their last resort, often ashamed, their grief compounded by feelings of having failed their loved one by not giving them a 'proper' funeral. The 'pauper's funeral' terminology of old doesn't help. Giving rise as it does to anxiety around what the service will look and feel like. This anxiety is partially justified as there is something of a postcode lottery in terms of service length, or even of having one altogether. Thankfully my council understands the importance of the ritual, providing a fifteen minute slot with a celebrant, and this goes some way to restoring a feeling of peace and dignity. I then spend the duration of the case walking the ever-shifting line between official, grief counsellor and friend, spending many hours of my own time chatting and texting. Never picking up the phone to relay information without first asking how the person is doing and then actually listening.

But we're getting too touchy feely, we are meant to be at the business end. You see how this job gets blurry, right? So, returning to my initial phone call, I will take as many details about the deceased as are readily available, this ranges from a lot in the case of family and care homes to sometimes zero in the case of police and coroner referrals. I will then drop everything else I am working on, as time is of the essence, and carry out some or all of the following tasks, depending on the case type. Instruct our funeral director to collect the body, go to their GP surgery to get their medical cause of death certificate, or phone the coroner to get the order for burial or cremation form, pick up their house keys from the police, visit our funeral director to schedule the date and sign the order, and then book myself a slot to register their demise.

To do this last bit I have to go to the online registration system where I am given the choice of either 'make a birth appointment' or 'make a death appointment'. Truly the circle of life. Making a death appointment grimly amused me at first, sounding as it did, like I was arranging a meeting with the actual grim reaper to complete the admin side of dying in his office. I stood up at my desk as I put my coat on to leave for my first ever registrar meeting and dramatically announced 'I must go, I have an appointment,' pause for effect, 'with death.' Putting the fun in funerals there. Of course, it's nothing as exciting as that and I simply collect the piece of paper which marks their official end, the death certificate. There are so many death certificates out there with my name on and giving my relationship to the deceased as 'causing the body to be burned/buried' that future historians searching local records will probably be wondering about me.

In between all of these appointments I will visit the deceased's residence and, in the case of those without family, carry out a house search with a view to finding any next of kin. They're usually hiding in address books, phone logs, a scrawled email address inside last year's balled-up Christmas card. They can also be extra hidden under years of hoarding or detritus. And sometimes just not there at all. In the absence of any immediate clues – hardly anyone has address books anymore and phones are so often pin-locked – I'll try knocking up the neighbours. And then if I find nothing, or I find something but none of the numbers lead anywhere and the emails bounce back, well, this is where things should end. There's nobody. Book the funeral, attend solo, and get back to work.

But whether it's through empathy, stockpiling karma, general nosiness, or a combo of all three, I can't let it end there. They must have been loved by someone or at the very least known to someone. And even if they somehow weren't, I can't just let them disappear. They deserve their decent farewell, their final summing up. So I also look out for clues as to exactly who they were, to help the celebrant tailor their funeral, and also because I genuinely want to know.

On top of looking for the usual wallets, bills, wills, bank statements with which to close down their life, I'm also looking for membership cards, letters, photos, diaries, evidence of hobbies, cd collections, signs of a religion and therefore preference for burial or burning. Any information to help me find, if not family, then friends, acquaintances, talents, ambitions, dreams, loves, lost loves: their life.

After I have taken a whistle-stop journey through their entire existence, I return to my public health duties and take their last ever meter readings, dispose of all perishable food, turn off the fridge and put their bin out one last time. Basically a cross between a private detective and a cleaning lady.

Then I take my evidence bag back to the office where I empty the person's life out onto my desk, flanked on all sides by similar desks taken up with the contrasting workaday admin that I would otherwise be doing if someone hadn't gone and died. Taxi plates being produced, premises licences being varied, someone taking a call about barking dogs, smelly drains, bonfire smoke, and of course the background buzz of people chatting away, most likely about Housing using our milk and tea bags again.

I put the papers in order – utility bills in one pile, bank statements in another, then credit cards, insurances, investments, pensions. I put the personal stuff to one side, as I'm going to start with the administrative things as a warm-up to the hard, human bit. I tell the DWP, I freeze their bank accounts, cancel cards, I listen to a whole lot of terrible hold music. In the case of credit card companies in particular I say 'something else' over and over again to a robot voice until it finally stops offering me unsuitable options and puts me through to a human. You can pay, you can transfer a balance, you can do anything, except die. I mean, why would you want to go and do that? If you're reading this, please do better, guys. Add a deceased account holder option early on.

I don't need to, but I go through their wallet and inform libraries, clubs, their store loyalty cards, so that the mailings cease and don't distress anyone, or waste paper if there's nobody around to distress. Fun fact, some stores let you bequeath points, I bestowed one chap's Clubcard balance to his brother-in-law. Then it's on to the strange task of calling random numbers in mobile phones and address books to inform whoever picks up of the death. It's daunting, because it could be a bemused plumber who did one job for them in 2014, or it could be the love of their life. You have to get very comfortable very quickly with being on the phone to people who are in shock and in tears. And often due to the nature of my cases, wracked with guilt. From the estranged family member who let things slide and is trying to justify themselves to me entirely unprompted, to the best friend who argued with them when last they spoke and kept asking me if I thought that's why they had committed suicide.

As I said earlier, if no family is found, it's over. But as I also said earlier, it's not over for me. If the phone calls don't pay off I will start trawling Facebook, Twitter, posting on local group pages and forums, using the personal clues I picked up in the house like a photo outside a pub, shop, cricket club, to track someone who knew them.

Sometimes it just comes down to desperate Googling of their name. It's amazing what you can turn up. One guy had an online tea shop and a section called 'The Old Tea Boy' which gave a run down of his entire life from his childhood in Ceylon, to his time as one of the youngest Brooke Bond trainees, driving around in the old fashioned red van, to his international tea-tasting career, covering every continent; all in his own chatty charming voice. A surreal experience, communing with the dead this way, but a warming one. By the way, I do this latter round of research on my lunch hour and then after-hours on my own time, as I am only paid to do the basic due diligence, and those taxi plates aren't going to make themselves; so at ease, taxpayer.

By the time the funeral arrives, my brief but intense immersion in the person's world causes me to feel as though I've met them and am attending myself as a friend. Indeed, when I was describing a couple of cases to someone recently they stopped me mid-sentence to say, 'it's like you know them and can see them in front of you'. True, I may never have met them whilst living, but their life and personality crystallized before my eyes during the carrying out of my basic duties, and my self-appointed ones too. Dead strangers are just friends you haven't met yet, that's what I say. I don't really.

On the actual day of the funeral, where there isn't family, the people I have found and corralled – friends, acquaintances, neighbours, carers and even the wider local community – will turn out to be there for them at the end, not out of familial duty, but out of wanting to be. Through this job I have learned something very comforting, that no-one truly has no-one. Not even anonymous unclaimed bodies as it turned out in one case. Good to know because there is another category of person, more common nowadays than ever before, who will almost certainly end up without a traditional family funeral; those who never had kids, and so when the time comes, will have no obvious person in line to dispose of them. This last category of person includes me, and may partially explain why I relate so much to my deceased people and try so hard for them. Don't get me wrong, I'm not sad about it. I once Tweeted: 'woke up at 11am, Curly Wurly for breakfast, now off to watch Buffy in the bath. Ask me again if I regret not having kids'. I still stand by that and will happily die alone on that hill.

Introduction

I hope that through this book I can shed some light on this little-known role, this job that operates in the margins, out of everyday sight. Not just for the sake of interest, intrigue or a good story, although these things inevitably get thrown into the bargain by the nature of events, but because people rather need to know about it.

The words 'you're going to die alone' are thrown out as the worst kind of insult, implying a life poorly lived, or a failed person. Those of us who are likely to face this outcome due to simple logistics are left feeling lumped into that category of people nobody loves, or even likes, and are left lying awake at three in the morning contemplating how long it will be before our body is found, or wincing at the idea of our under or unattended funeral. Well I am here to tell you that it's not how you die, are found, or are commemorated. Your life holds meaning whether it is laid to rest at a state funeral or with a Section 46. As I tell anyone who reacts to my job by saying 'how tragic', don't pity my people please, they lived a life. I mean, just look at the old tea boy.

I also hope that as we go along, I can impress the need for thinking about and preparing for our own endings. My many hours of rifling through drawers and cupboards to produce a still incomplete set of disorganised papers have been stressful enough, and I've not been saddled with the extra challenge of doing it whilst bereaved. We owe the people we leave behind a trail of breadcrumbs that allows them to close down our life as easily as possible at a time of high emotion and grief, or the beleaguered council worker some handy clues whilst working against the clock. A folder, a drawer, a notebook that lists it all; from who we bank with to how we want our body dealt with, therefore avoiding the grimmest of treasure hunts and the stress of decision-making at the hardest of times to think straight.

In order to respect those people connected to my cases who are still living and because it doesn't really matter who I technically am – my people are the stars here – I am writing this under an alias, a mega mix of my paternal and maternal grandmothers' first and last names. The combination of which makes for a much more authourish moniker than my own. It goes without saying that all other names have been changed too, even though the dead don't have any data protection rights. Another fun death fact for you there to file away with the gravestone one. Also a good alternative title for this book.

I have been truly privileged to be allowed into the homes, sock drawers and lives of these people. I have flicked through their vinyl collection, read their own words in notebooks, their last diary entries, disposed of their naked polaroids, uncovered lifelong secrets, stood in the room where they died, and now I invite you to join me there too, and go on the same journey I have been on.

And the best part is, you don't even need to wear a haz suit and shoe covers to do it.

Robert

This whole thing started, like many swashbuckling adventures before it, with me running away to sea. Though my reasons were considerably less exciting than Robinson Crusoe's.

I had started to find my city job, commute and home in the London 'burbs collectively unbearable, had developed a chronic pain condition after a collapse in my health due to the aforementioned, and had jacked it all in with only the sketchiest of plans; to live beside the seaside. See? Very sketchy.

When I left town I had one job interview lined up and an offer provisionally accepted on a house, otherwise known as no job and nowhere to live. I was that desperate to get away. I mean, when one of your neighbours is singing the confederate side version of the 'Battle Cry of Freedom' through the thin terraced walls it tends to put a fire under you.

Old problems left behind, I arrived and took on the new

one of having to shove my life into a storage container and live out of a suitcase in a spare room. I'd had no responses to any other applications so my one job interview at the council had a lot riding on it. Thankfully they offered it to me the same day, it was clearly meant for me, if I believed in that kind of thing, which as you know, I don't. It was especially good news as I had also just realised that I had left all of my socks in a drawer somewhere in that storage container, and I needed money to go on a frenzied hosiery spree.

With nowhere stable to live and fold marks permanently down the front of all my suitcase-stored clothes, but crucially nobody singing racist songs through a party wall – or ripping down the fence and digging up my garden when I was out, a story for another day, that – I started work. The expensive and delay-laden city commute full of loud businessmen on phones and people coughing in my face (back when that was considered just rude rather than an actual assault) was replaced by a walk along the beach, watching the sun coming up as I went, and dipping back down again on the way home. It was so freeing, living on the very edge of the world. I could breathe at last. Though Pizza Hut wouldn't deliver there and Deliveroo gave a nil return when I put my postcode in, but that's the high price of zen for you. As the majority of the town's population were retired, I was usually alone on these walks with nothing but the sound of the wind, the waves and the gulls. The seaside bit of my sketchy plan had come together beautifully, but would the job? Well obviously, or this book would end here.

The job itself started as an administrator post in the

environmental health and licensing team. I had deliberately gone for something entry level so I could guarantee the quiet life I had come down to find. It comprised, as I mentioned earlier, of trying to make changes to pub conditions and produce taxi licences and plates whilst fielding a steady stream of complaints about noise, smells, dogs, bonfires, poo, anything that annoyed people really, as well as redirecting dozens of erroneous enquiries about missed bins. FYI, you want waste, not environmental health; your bin isn't an environmental health issue unless it is full of asbestos that is on fire.

I sat in a pool of other administrators, who in turn sat next to a group of environmental health officers in an office that hadn't been refurbed since at least the 1970s – we're talking pink toilets and washbasins like the ones from The Shining here – it was very quaint, and things moved at a much more unhurried pace than the one I had come to escape from. The tense corporate open-plan silence of my old job was replaced by friendly chatter. People brought in veg from their garden to give away and home-baked goods to share, oh brave new world. As with every new job, I pretended I didn't like tea so I could swerve the endless Sisyphean rounds, and then settled in for that quiet life I mentioned earlier. The one we know I didn't get so I don't know why I am bothering to set it up.

A few weeks into the job, around the time I should have been completing, the housing chain I was in started to collapse. Wanting to be settled – and more importantly reunited with my socks – weekends and evenings were suddenly spent viewing exclusively empty properties to avoid another chain. The majority of these were on sale due to the death of an elderly owner who, as with my office toilets, hadn't done anything to them since 1972 and had left them with a signature musty smell. My endless tours of these deathly fire sale houses was strangely prescient in hindsight. Oh, look, there's some more of that cosmic significance I keep accidentally overlaying everything with, maybe I do believe. Anyway, nothing was remotely suitable and it was all becoming rather depressing. I kept it together at work though, maybe because you just have to, and also because it was my only solid ground. I only succumbed to the one morning off when my gums suddenly wouldn't stop bleeding. Good news, the dentist told me, there's nothing wrong with your teeth, it's caused by stress. Dental hygiene assurances are nice and all, but it wasn't the best good news I had ever received; you're bleeding profusely out of your mouth because of the sorry state of your life, huzzah.

As each viewing failed to offer even a glimmer of a new home, I accepted that I was stuck in the stalled chain for the time being and threw myself into the job, which I luckily quite liked. I mean in what other line of work do you get to field emails about 'a frightening encounter with a tinker'? The weird gripes in the inbox were like a daily soap opera, though sometimes more melodramatic. One complaint about light pollution set the scene, describing the source as 'several ugly blocks of flats, stark, white & red; as garish as an abstract barber's pole'. Strong imagery. They went on: 'every night the windows are illuminated by a stark yellow light, looming out of the darkness; it looks like the hovering spectre of a menacing Wendy House. Why?' Why indeed? Overuse of the word stark but otherwise good and atmospheric. Per our policy, I had to interrupt their one-man play to explain that we could only deal with light pollution where it shines directly into a property and could unfortunately not consider cosmetic complaints about light you can just see, looming out of the darkness, like a spectre. Their reply was on-brand dramatic: 'presumably then the answer is to move, or die.' I didn't know at the time that if they did the latter they could potentially end up back in the workload because, like most of us, I'd never heard of Section 46 funerals at this point.

I was being trained up by two different people on the environmental health side. Job-sharing part-timers who didn't get on and both had different ways of doing the same thing at their respective ends of the week, often without quite knowing why. Case in point, I was taught that when we did land charge searches on the computer we were also to write the results in a book. When I asked why, job-share woman number one didn't know.

'We just do it, always have,' she said.

Job-share woman number two said the same thing but didn't bother doing it for that very reason. One of the many things they butted heads over. When I asked around, it turned out the book predated the computer and should have been phased out when the new system launched, in about 1998, but job-share woman number one had held onto it. I decided to put a stop to this pointless duplication and drill down on a few other areas too whilst I was at it. In my previous job, every procedure was slavishly written down and signed off on to cast-iron ensure that the boss couldn't complain things were being done incorrectly when they weren't, not that this stopped him – a little glimpse into why I left for you there – so I, as a paranoid PTSD reflex, started taking notes of everything I was being shown and told, distilling the bits that made sense, dispensing of the bits that didn't and writing procedural guidance for each task to run past Cathy, my manager, to guarantee I was doing things correctly.

She was doing two senior management jobs at once after the head of another department left and was never replaced, and so was always open to someone taking the initiative to undertake things she wanted to make happen, but never had the time to coordinate, much less do. Pleased to have some sort of continuity and training notes, she read through them and clocked that I could write pretty well. Her words, not mine. (Though I don't know why I am wasting time being falsely modest about writing skills in my book.) I revealed that I had actually written professionally before and, realising she had slightly more than an administrator on her hands, asked me if I wanted to tackle a bigger task that needed the same treatment.

And so it began.

Section 46 funerals was an area lacking in any full written guidance and we were about to be audited. It was also an area that was wide open to abuse, involving as it did going into people's homes and handling any cash and valuables that were lying around. We really needed to be able to show our workings, to protect both the deceased's estate and ourselves. I was paired with Steve, an experienced environmental health officer who had also moved down from the city just months before me. This may have explained our immediate rapport, totally unconscious as we didn't learn this about each other until we were driving out to case number one. The shared sense of humour and demeanours helped too. He had been doing all of the funeral cases one-handed since the person responsible for the area had suddenly left, and had started on the guidance task but was too busy to finish it by himself.

EHOs get called out of the office all the time to stare into drainage ditches or ask people to stop playing the tuba at two in the morning, and so are very rarely at their desks. I took his draft procedure notes off him and in my quiet moments when I wasn't telling outraged locals, 'Sorry madam but the council has no power to compel anyone to change their curtains' and of course, 'Bins? You want the waste team', I worked them into a process. A month and a bit later I handed in my finished product, thinking I would then just return to my admin job.

'These are very good,' Cathy said. 'You seem to have a real grasp of this.'

Once again, her words, but once again, I clearly did as it's now my job so let's just agree to have no more falsely modest qualifying asides from here on.

'We've got some old funeral cases that need finishing up and closing down. How about Steve transfers them to you?'

I had written it up but the actual work felt way above my head, so I did the very British non-committal nod and shrug combo that could easily mean both yes and no.

'And then how about the next case that comes in, you go along, help Steve to test the procedure?'

I paused. 'Er, what, go to a dead person's house?'

She paused. 'Yes.'

Again I did the non-committal nod and shrug combo. I wasn't at all sure about this, but felt too new in the job to say no. And honestly, I was a little curious.

The leftover cases landed in my workload. I started to muddle through them, in between dealing with such enquiries as, 'Why does Ron the farmer have cows if he has no grass?', which sounded more like a riddle than a complaint and, 'Where have all the ducks gone?' I dunno, south?

These funerals had all long since gone ahead, but it was unclear as to where they were on the admin side of things. Steve had dealt with what he could, but there were a lot of notes to plough through in order to identify what his predecessor had done about the estates, if any, left behind. I gradually got to the bottom of each one, and as I read through the notes I flicked past eulogies, photos, details about the people's lives, before working out if the invoicing had been completed and they could be shut. It was a strange timeline. A life followed by an invoice request form, followed by the case closed justification of 'funeral arranged'.

After a couple of months of working from the safety of my desk on the finances and the written, and for the moment totally abstract, funeral procedure, a call was put through to my extension which ushered in the reality of the job. The coroner was on the line wanting to speak to someone about a deceased gentleman found in his home after the police were called by concerned neighbours. I remember fumbling around on my home drive for the annex-one information sheet Steve had designed to go with the guidance. It was to be used during the initial call to get all of the information we needed. I sat there opening and closing Word docs, all the while uh-huhing along to what they were saying and trying to sound like I had done this a thousand times before. Probably unconvincingly. Document found, I stopped stalling and started to field the details.

Right off the bat I was struck by how friendly and upbeat the coroner was, and then hot on the heels of that, struck by my own prejudice in expecting them to sound like, what, Lurch from the Addams Family? Of course they sounded normal, they were a normal person doing a normal job and this was a normal, daily occurrence.

Even though I was more than comfortable with death, having at one point wanted to be a funeral director as a child – an ambition then briefly replaced with truck driver, I think because of Pigeon Street's Long Distance Clara, and the proliferation of Happy Eaters along the motorways (showing my age now) – I still unconsciously held that embedded idea that many people do of the macabre morgue, the creepy undertaker. The same idea that people who sometimes wrinkle their noses when they hear what I now do and mention the words 'depressing' or 'morbid' hold. Understandably, perhaps, after years of drama shows and horror films drip feeding us this imagery.

My first lesson of the job was that those who work in the death industry are actually the least morbid people you will meet. It's those on the outside who see death through the lens of morbidity, due to the luxury, if you can really call it that, of being able to kick it out of their thoughts altogether, until one day it's suddenly upon them. Leaving it to lurk at the back of their minds all their lives like a dark – to quote my light pollution complainant – spectre.

As with the shadows in your bedroom at night, they disappear when you turn the light on, and those in the death industry work in the cold light of day, so death cannot lurk anywhere. Once out in the open it isn't so scary, like the curtain going up on the Wizard of Oz. This grand event, it's ordinary, part of the endless cycle of life. Seeing it so often, turning up at the crematorium and the board having six funerals listed for that day, watching hearses coming and going, the flowers from the last ten services slowly decaying in the garden, you'd think it would be enough to depress a person into a comatose state, but it's actually oddly comforting in its eventual mundanity.

It can also sometimes be ridiculous. And whilst I would never laugh at the way someone has died, hearing about a ridiculous death brings it into line with life where we mess up and embarrass ourselves frequently. It takes the sombre edge off and humanises things. I won't give you the example I am thinking of, because you will definitely judge me, but it was slapstick and tragic in equal measure and turned the grim reaper in my imagination from the one in The Seventh Seal to the one in Bill and Ted.

But however comfortable with the concept of death you become, you are never immune to the impact, because it's the people and the stories who present the existential and difficult stuff; that you can never get used to, because no one person or story is the same.

Anyway, back to me at my desk, hanging up the call and wandering off to find Steve and let him know we had a trip to the police station and a house search ahead of us. The funerals are just a small part of the larger job, and are by their very nature impossible to schedule so the call from the coroner is very much like the bat signal lighting up the night sky. We dropped all the other work we had on the go and scheduled for the next day. Before leaving the office that night we unlocked the department storage cupboard and put together some eye-opening supplies for the following day's excursion; evidence bags, shoe covers, haz suits, face masks, rubber gloves, Sharps kits, torches, all things more CSI than local council. What was I going to be walking into here?

In the morning after an ordinary start, clearing the emails, telling someone that slippery leaves in the park were not a public health risk, we left behind the buzz of the office to head to the police property store where the house keys were signed over to us in a sealed evidence bag. A mundane item packed up in the same way as a bloodied murder weapon, it was surreal, especially when I imagined them being used day in, day out. I wondered what the deceased would make of where they had ended up.

We then made the long drive to the edge of our district where this chap had lived. The house was located on a lovely country lane overlooking fields in a row of mostly picturesque properties with one exception: his. The front garden was impassable, completely overtaken by weeds and brambles. The front door too was out of use, three quarters of it covered in weeds and vines, like a grisly version of Sleeping Beauty. Water was pouring down the side of the house. My recent experiences having traumatised me a bit, I half expected to be greeted by an estate agent and told it had potential. We only had the one key and concluding that there was no way the front door had been used for at least a decade, we made our way around to the rear of the property and tried it in the back one.

As it swung open and we moved forward to enter the property we were physically pushed backwards by what I immediately came to know as the smell of death. If you're interested, it's a bit like someone was sick in a bucket of marzipan and left it in the sun for a week. It wasn't just a smell though, it was a thickness of the air, like opening an oven door and being struck in the face by the escaping heat.

We went back to the car and fetched the kit. Steve informed me that not every case required protective equipment, but this one likely would. I started to wonder what I was going to see in there. Walk through, handle, breathe in. How could I, an administrator, be expected to encounter whatever was waiting in there, raw and unsanitized? I don't know what I imagined happened at the scene of a death, mostly because I had never had to give it a moment's thought, but as I suited up I supposed it made sense that the police simply removed the body, that was their job over, and that the remaining scene – the staining where the person died, the fluids, flies, maggots, rotting food, all of this in some cases on top of years of pre-existing filth – remained. Remained for me to search through before the situation was passed to any family I found or, where there was nobody, contracted out to a specialist trauma cleaning firm. I started wishing I hadn't just done the nod shrug combo and had actually said 'thank you, but no'.

Suitably attired, we returned to the door where the smell was still spilling out into the cold fresh air. This time we entered with the same deliberate swiftness as you would when diving into a freezing swimming pool. Just hoping to get the initial shock out of the way and acclimatise.

I will never forget taking in the first room of my first house search. Even Steve, an experienced officer, was struck by the haunted house movie tableau presented to us. The thickest of thick cobwebs, like over-the-top Halloween decorations, holes in the ceiling, holes in the walls, filth on every surface, a once-white fridge covered in brown streaks, the leftovers of those final few meals sitting on the draining board, soup that now resembled solid gelatine, plates of meat animated by the movement of maggots, and a flashing, buzzing strip light above the water-filled sink with a tap drip, drip, dripping into it. It wasn't just the filth and the smell that was cloying though, it was what it clearly symbolised. The sadness of the scene enveloped me, the sadness of the fact that this repellent place that I was going to be barely tolerating for an hour through a face mask, was just weeks earlier, someone's life.

The first thing we had to do, after getting hit in the face by some y-fronts a few paces in, was to cut down a washing line that was criss-crossing the room, draping underpants in our eyeline. There was no washing machine, evidently this chap cleaned his smalls in the pot on the stove with the dirty water and the long wooden spoon sticking out of it, and from the colour of the pants, he clearly didn't use detergent. It was a mystery how he would have cleaned anything larger than his undies. I guessed he simply didn't. There was always the launderette I supposed, though the likelihood of this guy going on an errand to specifically clean things seemed slim.

As we stood there taking it all in, the silence was pierced by the letterbox flapping with the day's post which, thanks to the haunted house vibe, caused us to both jump ten feet in the air and let out a yelp each as we feared his ghost had come back to tell us not to be so judgy about his underwear. It also snapped us back into the job at hand and we stopped our staring and set about doing a recce of each room. The new guidance we had written stated that we had to be in each other's presence at all times so there could be no accusations of pilfering. Through we went, like children paired up on a terrible school trip, from the kitchen via the hall, passing on the other side of the impassable front door, and into a sitting room that was barely penetrable.

A small path ran through it, flanked on either side by tall piles of junk and upright painting canvases propped like half-fallen dominos. They were too close together to pry them apart and see the pictures, though there was one painting leaning against the wall on top of the stack. A giant oil rendition of a flower vase against a black background that somehow managed to be quite foreboding. It was signed Robert, the name of the deceased. Our man was an artist, it seemed.

The path through the sitting room led to a door to a back room where it abruptly stopped, blocked by yet more canvases that had been shoved in over many years until they were right up to the doorway, making the room completely impenetrable. Correction – our man was a prolific artist, and also a bit of a hoarder. Drowning himself in his own hobby, probably on purpose.

The back room was just a sea of these upright frames leaning against each other with some jutting up at angles like shark fins coming out of the deep. As before, they were too tightly packed to prise apart and there were only two pictures in this entire room that were facing us. One was a large oil painting of what appeared to be naked people in a row, possibly dancing. It was rendered in bright colours in a Picasso-esque cubist style, the faces distorted. As with the vase before it, I got a strange sense of unease from looking at it. Despite the vibrant colour palette, it had a darkness to it.

The other picture was much smaller, a head and shoulders portrait, no colour at all in this one. The background was pure black, the face was bright white with black shading, and the eyes were absent, just black holes, gaping sockets. I had no strange sense of unease over this one, just an obvious and clearly signposted one. I hoped he was just practising artistic styles because otherwise it spoke to him having been quite a troubled soul.

Unable to go forwards we backed up through the sitting room, stopping to comment on the incongruous pile of Vogue magazines stacked up on an armchair half hidden behind the canvases. There were no other chairs or sofas to be seen; he obviously did no sitting in this sitting room. Then back out into the hall and up the stairs we went, with great trepidation as after years of neglect the structure wasn't too sturdy and the kitchen could actually be glimpsed through gaps in the side of the steps.

The bathroom was the first stop on the landing and didn't appear to be in use. The toilet was blocked, the bidet smashed, the bath full of rubbish, no shower gel, deodorant, or bubble bath to be found. I caught a glimpse of myself in the mirror above the sink; it was discoloured and the glass was blown, covered in black spots. Seeing myself framed in this scene, in the mirror he would have looked in himself, gave me a shiver; the sensitive and intrusive nature of the job brought into sharp relief. His vanity table underneath was lost under a two-foot pile of chaotic miscellaneous detritus, none of it relevant to a bathroom. Bodily fluids stained the flooring to the extent that I thought it may have been the spot where he died. I edged out, feeling slightly sadder with every step.

The door next to the bathroom had a twee floral 'guest bedroom' sign on it, but by gloomy contrast was far from welcoming and again impassable, full to the doorway with junk that couldn't be clearly identified as the room was in almost pitch black, the bulb having long since died and the closed curtains on the other side of the room no longer able to be reached for opening. For how many years, I wondered.

The bedroom opposite was accessible and clearly Robert's own. No curtains in there, just a bit of thin, improvised material limply covering half of the window. Thick dust on every surface. Rubbish all over the floor, but no hoarding, no possessions of any kind in fact. He had no duvet cover or sheets, just a blanket on top of a bare mattress and a brown pillow that, like his fridge, used to be white.

The desolation of this room, a room where people retreat to feel cosy and comfortable, made us pause for a moment before we could move on with the search. Steve lifted the mattress of the bed where, he told me, Robert had clearly passed away. The bathroom stains must have been a sign of prior illness then I guessed, as he explained that these mattress stains were the real deal. In Steve's experience, many older people kept money under the mattress. In a previous case he had braved lifting one that was teeming with maggots and it was just as well he did, the lady's handbag was under there containing £8,000. Lifting Robert's mattress was an object lesson in wearing a face mask. There was a minimum of ten years' worth of dust under his bed, inches thick, that dislodged when the mattress was moved and flew up when it was dropped back into place.

I had only been there half an hour and I couldn't wait to leave. How had he lived like this for what looked like decades? I started to think back over all the things I had been doing in my own life down the years whilst he sat in this house. All of the Christmases, New Years, holidays, weekends that I had enjoyed. Had he been here all of that time sitting in cumulative dust, grime and silence? I presumed so anyway, having not seen a radio, and only glimpsed one old analogue TV buried behind the junk in the sitting room, opposite the out-of-use Vogue chair. Hopefully he had derived plenty of pleasure from his painting, or at least, what with all that foreboding, some sort of catharsis.

The final room clicked everything into place. The holes in the ceiling, walls and floors notwithstanding, it was a perfectly presented woman's bedroom. Pink silky bedspread, Victorian-style dressing table, pearl-backed hand glass, powder puff, Chanel No 5, necklaces draped across the mirror. The cobwebs and grime on top of this memory of a life gave it a feel of Miss Havisham's room and a transcendent glimpse back in time. The style and era of the items told us that it must have belonged to his mother. The stack of Vogue magazines downstairs suddenly made sense. This apparently glamorous woman was presumably a subscriber in life, and Robert must have kept it up as a comfort blanket when she died. It seemed to us that he had lived in the family home his whole life and had probably been unable to cope as he gradually lost his parents and was finally left alone. The house falling apart around him as he did so himself was quite poetic.

Whilst some clues brought everything into focus, one raised more questions than answers. At the end of his mother's bed there was a wooden platform with a huge professional stage light aimed at it. We looked at each other and kicked around theories. Maybe she was an actress or dreamed of being one. Maybe Robert performed for mother. The potentially cloying family dynamic conjured images for us of him tap dancing for her in a sailor suit well into his fifties. After a silent pause and a jokey shudder to lighten the pretty grim mood, we moved swiftly on.

It took an hour for us to complete the search and gather the necessary paperwork which, luckily for us, given the chaos and hoarding, had been helpfully stored in the kitchen dresser. Even the paperwork that had been contained in drawers had managed to become caked in years of insistent dust. We then collected the post that had so startled us earlier from off the mat and scooped up a pile from the kitchen table in case anything significant had arrived in the past weeks.

Our initial hunch was that there was no next of kin to be found here, and if there were, the stacks of rubbish could make it challenging to find them. For the moment, we made do with one phone number written on a scrap of paper sitting in a fruitless fruit bowl. There was also a photo in there of a man with his arm around a bikini-clad woman at what looked like a Hi-de-Hi!-era holiday camp. The man had a facial disfigurement. Then another photo underneath that.

The man with the facial disfigurement and two older people, male and female, standing outside the front door, we had been unable to use. In the photo, the door was pristine, painted bright blue, and the path to it was clear. The older couple were most likely the parents. The chap with the facial disfigurement, Robert. Perhaps this explained his hermit lifestyle and the disturbing faces in his paintings. I was glad to see that this place had once been a happy home for him, and hoped that he had been inhabiting that memory all of this time.

Evidence bags filled and sealed we cleared away the putrid food, emptied the fridge, put out the bins and turned off the water to stop any further damage to the house. As we were locking up, a curious neighbour saved us a door knock and came up the path – there's always a curious neighbour, Steve told me – and corroborated the facts behind the scene we had just stepped out of. Robert had lived at home his whole life, he was a shy man, a mother's boy, you would see him in the back of his parents' car, a perpetual child. His father was a big deal in the area, owning a stake in a local newspaper, they were very well off. His parents predeceased him by a couple of decades and he had become reclusive. There were no regular visitors apart from the butcher making deliveries. In recent years she had been concerned for his mental state, but didn't know who to tell. A few months ago he had walked down the lane naked, she said.

We took everything back to the office where everyone fired off questions about how it went, what we had seen, if we had found any clues, all of which I fielded in something of a fugue state. Before I did anything else, I went for my lunch break, if only to take a quiet moment and process everything I had just seen. Marinating in that environment for an hour, it had stayed with me, clung to me, and I needed to walk myself out of that headspace.

I wandered around the shops in a daze, the headache I had been brewing all day coming to the fore, body aches and fatigue setting in from being on my feet all morning. I tried to find something to eat that took my fancy, but the feeling wasn't the only thing clinging on, the smell of death was stuck in my nostrils. I had really bad hunger pangs but was simultaneously nauseous, so just went ahead and bought a sandwich that I didn't want, which I barely touched. The same thing happened that night with dinner. The smell of death was still there when I got home. Still there after my shower. I was convinced it was all over my skin. I asked people to smell me, they couldn't detect anything. After I established they weren't just being diplomatic, I realised it was all in my nostrils, maybe in my head too. Thankfully it was gone by morning. As interesting as it had been to see the house and play detective, I really didn't fancy doing it again. It was grimy and hard and way above my pay grade and I planned to diplomatically tell Cathy so at our next one-to-one.

Back at my desk, amidst another tea round and talk of making laminated signs to warn Housing off our stash, I started to look through Robert's post, kicking off with his bank statement. Wow. My first case was turning out to be a potentially complex one. There was a large estate here, hundreds of thousands of pounds in his current account and presumably he owned the house too. Filthy rich but living in filth. What a waste. This type of thing was apparently quite common. Another colleague would later tell me about a case of hers concerning an old man who lived in one room of his mansion, sitting and sleeping in one chair. He would walk to the shops, buy a ready meal or sandwich, eat it, drop the packaging on the floor to one side of the chair, and then on the other the, ahem, output; piles of freezer bags containing his excrement. He had millions in the bank.

If we didn't find any useful leads from the paperwork we'd recovered, we would need to search the house again more carefully to find next of kin to hand the sizeable estate over to. Actually going through those piles of rubbish we had climbed over and around before. Because if nobody could be traced we would have to arrange to clear the house of rubbish, take any items of value to auction, add those monies to the estate and then refer the whole case to the Government Treasury Solicitor. That's right, if there is nobody to inherit your money, it goes to the man or, if you live in Cornwall, Prince William*. True fact, Google it, I'll wait... weird, right? So do make a will and leave it to a favourite charity if you've no family.

But before climbing this mountain, Steve first tried the one and only phone number we had found. And that's where Robert's story, like the path through his sitting room, abruptly stops, or rather where it diverges away from my own again.

To our incredible surprise and relief, the person who answered was family. A cousin who, despite rarely speaking with him, was not only saddened by the news, but willing to take the funeral arrangements and the estate away from us. They had put the piece of paper with their number on it through the door in an effort to reach out. He hadn't responded, they told Steve mournfully, but at least it had eventually reunited them, in a way. The relief at his sad life – towards the end at least, because surely the shadow

---

* Previously Prince Charles. The Queen's death occurred during the final edit of this book. The editor's note was 'change Charles to William'. My response was 'plus ça change Charles to William more like' as the archaic right passed down, along with first dibs on any shipwreck.

of grief was cast by the loss of a truly happy beginning – ending with a family funeral, was a satisfying end, vaguely cheerful even. The eulogy, though I would never hear it, would surely contain stories from the time when that front door was painted bright blue and able to be opened. I only got to see the sad outcome, but that didn't invalidate the beginning.

Then just as Robert's files were packed up and handed back to his family, the phone rang again. Thankfully I was in a much better position going into my next case as, 130 days after packing up and moving, I had a house to actually take my packed-up items and move into. My gums had stopped bleeding and I'd even had the time and headspace to return to London for a weekend at a friend's house after being more or less paralysed all those months by desperate house viewings and the inertia of anxious waiting.

My trip back was for a taxidermy class; death at work, death on the weekend – albeit mouse death – I was clearly being courted by the grim reaper. I had bought it for my friend with whom I had been having a weird birthday gifting competition that had gotten out of control. It had seemed like a whimsical idea at the time of booking, but then it's all fun and games until you have a dead rodent and a scalpel put in front of you. (I should say, before you all write in, that the mice came from the freezer section of a pet store and were intended to feed snakes, so they weren't killed for the class, though they were used for a more frivolous purpose admittedly.)

We were walked through the process by a quite bored and

unhelpful tutor. Any questions were met with a gentle sigh and a slight eye roll; she seemed to think it should all be rather obvious. I suppose when you cut open, disembowel and stuff animals all day every day you can take this stuff for granted.

First we were instructed to make an incision down the middle of the belly, not too heavy though, so as to leave the membrane holding the guts together intact. She said this bit slightly too late for me. I duly split my membrane, and had a bloodied mouse with entrails sticking out. I decided to style it out when I posed him, call it a zombie theme. Then we were told to use the scalpel to loosen the innards and set them aside – I am aware that this is starting to sound like a very strange cake recipe.

Finally we used the size and shape of the real innards as a template for making our replacement ones. Fashioned out of straw, shaped, tried on by the mouse to see if they needed adjustments, and then bound with string before stuffing into the skin and finally sewing the mouse back up.

I am in no way good with my hands, so my mouse's legs were pointing the wrong way and the stitching was horrendously visible, Frankenstein's monster-esque. It fit the zombie theme though.

My handiwork was so hideous that my friend ended up doing a laugh that became maniacal then morphed into a kind of crying and shaking before returning to a final guffaw. Happy birthday.

When I returned to work the next week, the dust having settled on the house search trauma and a stomach-strengthening mouse disembowelment under my belt, I held back on telling Cathy I wasn't really up for this job.

Having reunited Robert with his family and seeing the potential for putting a positive end to these situations, I was now on the fence. And the case that was called in next would get me off the fence altogether and stop me from ever wanting to have that conversation again.

Enter, Jean.

Jean

I moved into my new home the day before my birthday, delighted to have just squeaked through before having symbolically aged another year whilst waiting. Between having to pay to move twice, then shelling out for storage in between times, I was tight for cash to say the least. I didn't have much furniture. Most of it was at the end of its life when I moved and it would have made no sense to pay someone to drive it 100 miles and then pay someone else to store it, so apart from my bed and a few other bits, I came pretty much empty-handed. No house, no job, and also practically no furniture, yes, that was one sketchy plan. Mostly because it was pushed through in haste and pretty much by accident.

I was declining a meeting from my previous manager at what was to be our new Canary Wharf offices and after the usual qualifying response about being busy, my hands just kept typing and somehow meandered into an observation that it would add a grand to my already two and a half grand commute to a job I hated, so I guess, I quit? I pressed send before I had really registered what I'd typed and realised there was no going back on it. I was on the property sites by lunchtime.

I bought a sofa on the never-never so I would at least have somewhere to sit and left my moving boxes in the empty half of the kitchen where the dining table that I had yet to own would one day go. My old house didn't have room for a dinner table; I ate off my lap for seven years. I was now nearly a grown-up, I had space for a table, if not a table itself, this was progress. I had nothing to empty the dining room moving boxes into as my old place had made up for being teeny-tiny by having loads of cupboards built into every nook and cranny, so I had never bought any storage. This new place was bigger and the rooms were bare; no wardrobes, no recesses, no shelves. I had no money to make these things happen either. I needed to magic some up.

I cracked open one moving box and emptied out all of my old Sega Megadrive and Super Nintendo games. If I wanted a grown-up table I would need to sell my childhood toys. And boy did they sell. Two grand I got in the end. See, Mum, it was a clever investment strategy all along. Then as I drove to the post office, one cold but sunny Saturday morning, to send off the packaged up cartridges to other nostalgic '80s kids, thinking happily about how I was settled at last and had a wedge of cash to do a bit of nesting with, someone jumped a stop sign at 40mph and ploughed into my driver's door. Obviously. The timing would have been comical if it hadn't been so terrifying and slightly persecution complex-inducing.

I sat there in shock for a minute, still and silent, until my mind started slowly whirring again. It's funny what you think about in a crisis. I was on a plane once that started diving. And then kept diving. I remember looking around and watching people go from wondering what was happening to believing they were about to die. Overhead lockers fell open and bags pelted down. Items flew off tray tables. Window shades snapped up as people, formerly dozing in night mode, opened them to see what was going on, and light shafts cut across the fuselage like lasers. I sat there, zen as you like, and my last thought on this earth had there been a crash that day would have been: 'Lucky I finished my orange juice or it would have spilled all over my trousers.' Nice to know I will calmly embrace death in all its banality. Similarly, as I sat there in the wreckage, I just thought about how unlikely it would be that I would now get to the post office.

Boring gateway thought completed and I was back in the room, pondering about how this would be my whole weekend now and would impact the weeks ahead, maybe months if it was a write-off. Just as I had got straight too. A month since moving in, since regaining stability. A month's grace, that was really all I was getting?

Well and truly returned to the moment thanks to my anger, I flipped back to my practical brain and realised I needed to clear the road and pull over. Desperate for the situation not to be as it clearly was, I found myself hoping that maybe despite the force and the huge crunch it was just a ding. The sound of my car scraping along the tarmac, and the hideous creak of the wheels trying to turn inside the mess of crushed metal, confirmed the dismal fact that it was quite a bit more than that and I wouldn't be going to the post office today, or indeed anywhere in this car for a long time, if ever again.

The driver, an elderly lady, got out and was surprisingly belligerent for someone who had just caused a major accident. Too taken aback at her attitude to say much I just stood there as she talked at me and, inadvertently, herself into a corner. We swiftly went from a fleeting perfunctory accusation of my going too fast, that even she didn't seem to believe, to an irritable admission, as though I had pestered it out of her that ok, yes, she didn't stop or look, but still, she never looked, she left that to her husband and it had never been a problem before in all her many years of impeccable driving, I'll have you know.

It was quite something, having this woman who had just wrecked my car and my newly-found contentment detain me for a quarter of an hour to tell me about her great driving record, to take hold of my arm at one point and instruct me to stop shaking from shock and get over it, before passively aggressively telling me that I didn't have the monopoly on being upset about this, mine wasn't the only car that had been damaged. I had some serious spirit of the stairway about not telling her I had an actual right to be annoyed about my damage because I didn't do it to myself by driving into someone else at speed. But I didn't want to be waylaid any further by engaging with this harbinger of my ongoing existential inertia, so I stopped her mid-flow and asked to simply exchange details please so I could arrange a tow truck and go back to bed. Whilst waiting for the rescue vehicle to take me home I took some photos of the scene, of the two giant stop signs, and of the thick white lines on the road where she should have braked and waited. She watched from a distance, seemingly noticing for the first time the things she had blasted past, and then approached me before I got in the lorry to pointlessly say that she, irrespective of whose fault it was (subtext, hers), wouldn't be apologising to me because these things happen, dear. Only if you drive through stop signs without looking, dear.

The rescue vehicle unloaded my car onto the drive where it heaved and collapsed into position as though exhausted and mildly depressed. I knew how it felt. I paid my pricey out-of-hours rescue fee, seethed at the fact that some of my new-found money had been eaten into by this nonsense, and then went inside, steeling myself for a combative afternoon of fighting my corner with insurance companies; primed to submit my crime scene photos, compose long defensive emails and bat back her preposterous defences.

First things first, though, I put the kettle on to prepare the traditional English beverage of calamity, a cup of sweet tea – busted, I do drink it – but before it had even boiled, the phone rang. I was fairly delirious as her insurer told me that she was one hundred per cent at fault and would I like a courtesy car until mine was fixed or replaced, plus a refund on the flatbed lorry and any taxis I needed to take before the courtesy car arrived, oh and also some physiotherapy and compensation too? Having to simply say 'er, yes please' was a huge relief, but also a strange comedown which left me with a surplus of kinetic energy in my belly for a fight I no longer needed to have.

I wondered if she had reflected when she got home and realised she had been in the wrong. Of course not. The call centre chap explained that she had detailed her time-honoured driving method of not looking at junctions and in addition to this defence, which she didn't realise was actually a case for the prosecution, he had then taken one look at the road layout before telling her that she was bang to rights and then hanging up to tell everyone else in the office about the most bananas claims call he had ever had.

I sat there on my interest-free sofa all weekend as the shock wore off and the pain kicked in. Furniture shopping was put on hold and the only thing I managed to get done through the pain was emailing eBayers to explain the reason for the delay. I had some excellent feedback when the parcels actually got sent, referencing my good comms even in adversity.

The pain got worse by the hour. An underscore of dull throbs overlaid with sharp stabs. A headache that painkillers couldn't touch, a neck so stiff that I had to turn my full body to look behind me. I was unable to extend my arms to dress myself or to put my coat on without crying, pain exploding from the centre of my back outwards, as though my rib cage was conducting it. At least it masked my normal everyday pain, every cloud...

In my sorry state I limped back to work on the Monday morning to that next death call being put through to my extension.

It was actually a welcome distraction in one respect, something bigger than myself and my petty earthly problems to focus on. And it was somehow slightly less dismal than the first email I saw in the environmental health inbox that day concerning someone regularly defecating in a local bus shelter. The dead don't do that, they are model citizens. But I was still wavering and it was with some trepidation that I took the case on. Where would I end up this time? I pictured a similar scene, similar smells, all overlaid with a finishing touch of personal tragedy. I wasn't overly squeamish but could I really keep wading through bodily fluids, grime and, more crucially, any associated sadness long term?

Thankfully, Jean gave me some temporary respite from this dilemma by very considerately living, and dying, in a residential care home.

Such cases, I quickly came to learn, were naturally easier on two fronts. First, no house to search, simply one well-kept room with a couple of drawer sets and a bedside cupboard. Not even that sometimes. Homes are often so keen to continue the revenue stream and get a new occupant through the front door that you turn up and get handed a couple of carrier bags from the deceased's already emptied room; someone's life in a bag for life, deep. As supportive as I am of death-positive minimalism, to the point where I no longer buy non-useful 'stuff' because it's all just got to be thrown away when I die, it's quite arresting the first time you take possession of the sum total of a person's existence in such a stripped down and unceremonious way. This mildly unsettling feeling is also typically compounded by the low calibre of the contents. The things they owned in life, that they adorned their homes with, that would give clues to their character, are absent, long gone, with only practical items following them to their final residence; denture paste, clothes, incontinence underwear, a Twix and a puzzle book or two.

Second, you get a literal cheat sheet with basic information about the deceased documented neatly therein. Accordingly there's less detective work required than turning over an entire house, just pull the care plan from the filing cabinet and scan a copy of the 'about me' page; a mini-interview care homes do with the service user when they take them on which asks for their favourite food, music, TV shows and sometimes more, like people and memories. I had seen one of these on an old funeral file when I had been closing down Steve's inherited cases. There had clearly been some family estrangement as the lady had given the politician's answer of 'no comment' to the 'any children' question. She had then answered the 'any grandchildren' question with 'don't know' which kind of blew her cover.

As with the bag of items though, these questions are not always the most revealing and you end up with only a surface-level glimpse, finding yourself reliant on other residents and the nursing staff. The former group are often too incapacitated, ill or asleep to get to know their fellow housemates and the latter group are often too busy, spread too thin or – due to high turnover or reliance on agency workers – not there long enough to build bonds. Though sometimes you can get lucky as indeed we did with Jean's belongings and staff intel.

Jean's carer seated us in the dining room, just off the day room from where the daytime sounds of Bargain Hunt floated through. The, what I would come to know as traditional, carrier bags were handed over and the care file placed on the table. We were left there with a cup of tea – busted twice, flagrantly drinking it again – whilst the carer went off to see to a couple of people.

Steve looked through the bags, I leafed through the care plan. According to Jean's cheat sheet, she had been at the home for nearly forty years, before records began. Well that couldn't be right. I scribbled the number on my notepad with a question mark next to it, to remind me to ask the carer when they came back. She liked Cash in the Attic. That was coincidentally up next on the telly next door, where Jean would have sat day in, day out, so it was probably less of a preference and more Stockholm syndrome, definitely not worth mentioning in the eulogy, unless we got very desperate indeed. Her favourite people were all noted as deceased, their names crossed through like some sort of hit list. Their relationship to her was given as brother, friend and cousin. She had evidently, at 99 years old, outlived everyone. A downside to longevity that people sometimes don't consider, and something that is striven for blindly in our life-at-all-costs culture. There's life and there's just being alive. The two things are like axes on a graph and need to be considered equally in the scramble to just simply not be dead.

When the carer came back through, I asked if they were aware of any other family or had observed any regular visitors. No other family and no visitors since the brother, who came to see her every Christmas, had passed away. Jean had never married or had any children, the family line stopped with her. Jean was basically me in half a century's time I thought, without any sadness, as it was no reflection on either of us.

The carer sat back down at the table, and from the deep sigh she let out it was clearly the first time she had been off her feet all day. The sigh also had an air of dejection. As used to the deaths of her charges as she was, these being an occupational hazard, there was still some sadness when the inevitable happened. She opened right up, as I have come to find that almost everyone does in the aftermath of a death. Death is so profound, bemusing, existential, distressing, that it obliterates small talk and raises the conversation far and above the norm. When people answer the phone to me and hear the news they will often, entirely unprompted, immediately spill everything; good, bad and ugly. As the job goes on, I find that spending so much of my time inhabiting this hinterland where the usual rules and walls are gone, has left me permanently open. This proves to be both good and bad for me; far less bullshit but much more crying.

We chatted about Jean over tea like friends at her wake. Her story was a familiar one. The reason she had entered care almost four decades earlier, pre-dating the records, was that, like Robert, she had lived in the family home her whole life and upon losing her mother at the age of 59 had been entirely unable to cope. I was only two cases in but there was a through line developing here. Lives so tied up in one relationship that they ceased to mean anything without that counterpoint, collapsing inwards and forming a black hole. There was a slight divergence however. Whereas Robert's home decayed around him, Jean's grew around her. The property we were sitting in at that moment had been owned by her family, and had slowly been turned into a care home around Jean, the inaugural resident. Suddenly her long tenure in care didn't seem quite so bad. The alternative would most likely have been Robert's situation, living like a ghost in a life long gone, all alone. At least she had company and singalongs and bingo nights.

We had established that there were no surviving family but wanting to know more, perhaps because one day it would be my own life that risked going unremarked upon, I asked what she was actually like. Thankfully the carer had worked there long enough to have something to tell us and Jean had been there so long she had a legendary status that preceded her. When I went back to the home for another case a year later the new manager who had started six months after her death had heard of her. And here's why. She insisted on ice cream for lunch every single day. This, along with never marrying, was clearly the secret to a long life.

She also had a grapefruit every morning for breakfast which she refused to eat with cutlery, preferring to shove it straight into her face and gnaw the contents until the skin was empty, apparently a sight to behold.

A CQC inspector had been present at breakfast once and had commented disapprovingly that Jean had not been provided with any cutlery. The carer had explained that she would just refuse it, but the inspector pressed their case and a spoon was put next to the grapefruit bowl. Jean pushed the spoon away, went with her usual method and the inspector admitted defeat; big up Jean. Formerly she would follow her morning grapefruit with a few cigarettes but she decided to give up smoking aged 90, presumably because it can cut your life short.

By this point I had already decided that Jean was my spirit animal but the two bags we took away confirmed this further, thankfully holding within them more than denture paste and even more of her unique and lovable character. I poured the contents out onto my desk back at the office where the laminated signs were now up and in all caps, a clear declaration of war. I was so glad I had swerved tea club and could just drink water and be Switzerland.

Apart from one bank book with a 75p balance and a closed savings account statement there was nothing financial or legal, just photos of her one and only holiday to Spain – the favourite memory from her cheat sheet, taken with the cousin whose name I had seen crossed through on her favourite people list – and pages and pages of writing, mostly poems. Wonderful, I thought, I already have some anecdotes about her to use in her eulogy, but now I also have some stirring poems to read out, penned by the deceased herself, funeral gold.

This vision of a moving funereal moment stalled slightly as the first few I read were about a man who had flashed her, a friend with dementia who kept imaginary chickens and an ode to losing her favourite pair of knickers. Rather unsuitable for a funeral, I thought, or possibly very suitable depending on how you looked at it, thoroughly reflective of her obvious eccentricity after all. I set them to one side, put a pin in that idea and read on.

She had grouped her writing into categories and there were lots of poems in one bundle about the seasons and beauty in nature, much more traditionally funeral suitable, so I picked out a few of those for the priest or celebrant to choose from. I then found one in a more personal section about herself and her life called Writer's Lament, describing how she had always wanted to be published but never had any interest and how it had deeply wounded her. That one obviously went straight onto the yes pile; it both told a story about her and would put that situation to rights by having her poem read out in public, albeit at her own funeral, but true genius is never appreciated in its own lifetime, right Jean?

This personal section also included an adorable ode to a gentleman asking if he could walk her up the local high street. In the poem they walked the entire length and a fleeting connection was made, possibly romantic. She then gave me a bonus laugh as I turned the page and saw that on the back of the poem she had written a note: '…we didn't walk the entire length of the high street, poet's licence'.

This section of personal poetry was followed by one piece of prose she had written when her mother had died that reinforced what her carer had told us about her being unable to face life alone: 'The world opened up and swallowed me and I was suddenly bereft of the very best friend I ever had. I immediately brewed myself some hot, sweet tea to ward off the shock, then another, and another.' Having just recently used the hot sweet tea method myself I felt a very real connection with her in that moment.

I put everything back in the bag and concluded that as there were clearly no loose ends, and no next of kin to be found here, the funeral definitely fell to the council. I made my death appointment, and that awesome joke before leaving the office, and then booked her big day. Celebrant confirmed, I scanned the poems and emailed them across to him. I then told the care home the date in the hope that they could send people along, maybe bus in the old folks. It didn't seem fair that the reward for a long life was an empty chapel by default, especially in the case of this grapefruit-scoffing legend. I wished I knew more about her, but the modern day carer anecdotes and the selective poems and prose were all I could glimpse. Facts and stories from her childhood, youth, prime of her life, were all lost to time. And from the sounds of her, they would have been very interesting. A real pity.

My work on her case completed, I returned to my other duties – like telling the woman off the Hotel Inspector that she had erroneously filled in a minor variation form instead of a transfer; razzle dazzle – fully expecting to think no more of it until the day itself, but in the margins of my job and my life outside of it, I found myself gradually getting nervous as it approached. This wasn't my first rodeo, I had been to a few family funerals, but it was my first of this kind. How would it feel? How was I supposed to act? To dress?

Not knowing what else to do, I came to work the day-of, wearing all black and spent the morning doing light admin whilst dressed as a Victorian mourner.

At lunchtime I headed over to the crematorium. Jean may have had no family or friends left, but I was relieved to see that she wasn't going out alone. The care home staff were thankfully there, waiting outside the chapel in their work gear, having been allowed out for an hour. They don't always come. With the amount of deaths in their line of work they can't afford to attend every funeral nor could the homes logistically cope with it if they did, so Jean had clearly made an impression on them. We stood there waiting for her, one council worker in all black and three carers in all-blue scrubs, an odd scene that I think she would have found amusing.

An official but kind-looking man was standing in the chapel entrance. He was either a crematorium worker or our celebrant, so I edged towards him and eventually chanced saying the name of the man I had been emailing all of Jean's poetry and prose to: Martin. He smiled and nodded.

'Ah, and you must be Evelyn? Thank you so much for all of the information, it's far more than I would usually get for a council funeral.'

He then cited the example of a service he had done the day before where the only fact about the deceased had been provided by his solicitor: he liked football, I think. Perhaps he had just been tasked with council funerals for those with no clues remaining about them. This seemed odd though. A cursory glance around Robert's house had told me that his mother was important to him and that he loved art. A quick rummage in Joan's carrier bag revealed her writer chops. His surprise at what he called my efforts, which hadn't been much, made me realise I had done much more for Jean than possibly would have been done for her if she'd hit someone else's desk. His resulting eulogy would be the payoff that made me fall in love with the job, or rather what the job could be.

The hearse arrived and I recognised the person walking slowly out in front of it as Jodie, the young woman who I had sat down with in the funeral director's weeks before to book the service. Another stupidly surprising first. The office wasn't staid and sombre, but bright and homely, staffed by friendly, bubbly people who dealt with the dead with good humour and deep respect in equal measure. They too had been surprised at how invested I had been in Jean. I was surprised at their surprise. How could you not be? Oh very easily, they had replied, with examples from other such funerals. She gave a subtle smile of recognition as she edged past me and then suddenly to my right, a row of smartly dressed men appeared, the bearers.

Jodie joined the row and they, along with Martin, bowed as the hearse came to a stop. I joined in, a bit late, and was bobbing back up as they stepped forward to lift Jean out. I was pleased to see a spray of flowers on top of her coffin, provided by the care home owners. I was also strangely affected by the sight of this coffin containing the woman whose poems I had been reading and whose personality I'd heard so much about. She suddenly became three-dimensional and, as odd as it sounds, it was like meeting her in person for the first time, like a Twitter acquaintance or a French pen pal.

The other thing that struck me during this peculiar rush

of emotion was how much everything looked and felt like a 'proper' funeral. The 'pauper's funeral' label attached to council services had conjured up preconceived images of everything being horribly basic, almost deliberately spartan and bare, just to make the spiteful point that this wasn't the real deal. Well, not a bit of it. The coffin, whilst the most economical model, yes, was actually quite nice and thanks to the added flowers it looked the business.

Jodie, dressed in her full grand attire – top hat wrapped with a sash, long jacket with silk waistcoat – bowed again as the coffin was carried past her by the bearers into what was a lovely little chapel. Jean was carefully placed on an elegant stand alongside Martin as the 'White Cliffs of Dover' played us in, a song suggested by her primary carer who had told us that Jean loved to hear this tune from her youth at the music nights in the home. As the bearers left the chapel, they bowed to her one more time whilst the music faded in step with their departure. As I watched all of this, everything suddenly became very real. What had started with a referral form had resulted, via all of the associated admin, in this very authentic and human moment.

I hadn't expected to be moved by the ceremony of this woman whom I'd never met and who'd had, by all accounts, a very good innings, but as Martin talked about her, using the information I had taken the time to find, bringing her back to life in the room, causing nods of recognition and tears from her carers, I realised the impact this work could have. Then when 'Amazing Grace' was played during the mid-service period of reflection I suddenly had to concentrate very hard on not crying myself. Weirded out, I stared at the carpet, tried to think mundane thoughts, blinked excessively as though attempting to fan my eyes dry. What was happening here? Thankfully as the track faded, I found that Jean's poem about her knickers had made the cut and it brought me back to some sort of equilibrium. Here it is by the way:

Where have my pink knickers gone?
I had them yesterday morning
I forgot to put them on
And then there was this dawning
I looked beneath my bedroom chair
They're not hidden in the washin'
I looked inside my chest of drawers
But that is where they're not in!
I'll have to have another look
Penny put them in a drawer
At least that's what I've just been told
But no, they're still not there!
I found them in the wardrobe –
Why didn't I look inside?
Never mind, at last they're found
They are my joy and pride!

There you go Jeanie, published at last.

Whilst the ode to knickers, fun food facts and her own words about her mother had gone some way to person-alising the service, there were of course notable gaps that nobody was left to fill. Her genesis story was entirely missing.

All we knew was that her life had effectively ended upon her mother's death. But not what that life had constituted before then. Martin worked deftly around this challenge by hooking the first paragraph of the eulogy to her date of birth and the historical events she was born into and grew into a young woman throughout; two world wars. Extrapolating that she would have lived through hardships and then linking back to what we did know; that she enjoyed the war time music of Vera Lynn. He namechecked her favourite people but could go no further as the care home questionnaire didn't have room for why they were important, just boxes to list them in. All the stories contained in those relationships, gone forever.

I cheered myself up by concluding that this wasn't a comment on her life. Not hearing her story didn't mean she didn't have one. With her personality, how could she not? I then thought back to Robert and remembered how I'd had a similar thought and, realising that if I'd been tasked with looking into him further, I would have found stories there too. Everyone has a story.

As the service ended, the curtain slowly closed around her coffin, literally the final curtain falling on her life. As it did so 'We'll Meet Again' struck up, another of her favourites, and a poignant one at that, to end a funeral and a life on. Between the imagery and the song, I had another wobble and said a hurried goodbye to Martin and Jodie so that I didn't cry in front of them.

I then spent the drive back to the office blubbering and moving away from my initial concerns about grimy house searches to questioning out loud my ability to do this job even if I wanted to. The searches were physically difficult but the connections would be emotionally difficult, which was way harder. I pulled up in the car park, composed myself and reflected. The reason I was crying was because I had got to know this person. By reading her poetry and trying to understand her life, I had come to like her. It had been a privilege and not something I wanted to get out of anymore.

The house searches I could get used to and as for the emotional stuff, I would just have to find a way to retain my connection to these people in order to do right by them, but create enough of a disconnect to not become a permanent basket case. Hopefully that would come with time. A friend joked when I started writing this book that the final chapter would simply read 'some bloke died, buried him.' Hopefully I won't go that far the other way, I said. Stay tuned to find out.

Back at my desk, styling out my puffy eyes as pain-related, I got back down to work. A strange adjustment from a chapel of rest to a desk, ticking the 'funeral arranged' box on the case file and returning to licence processing and responding to miscellaneous queries and rants. And when I say miscellaneous, I mean it. Alongside the usual bins and dog poo, I had one about 'loud badinage' – surely if there's badinage afoot you want to be able to hear it clearly? – and an enquiry about what to do with the cat that was living next door by itself after the owner had died and left it the house. The caller had been popping in to feed him for four years but now the house was starting to deteriorate because Mr Cat didn't do much towards the upkeep. All of this helped to re-centre me again after quite an existential morning, but also concurrently made me crave the peace and quiet of my funeral case once more.

These calls were the stuff of life; and life was so much noise. I found myself looking forward to my next call, not to someone dying obviously – I've had this conversation with the registrar, funeral director and celebrant, and we always carefully caveat 'hope to see you again soon' with 'not that I am wishing anyone dead of course' – but die they will, whoever they are, out there right now, wandering around, as unaware of me as I am of them, but about to become the focus of my life for weeks on end.

And as I had done for Jean, I would do my best for them too; try to find out who they really were and ensure their last hurrah befitted them, to find their story and make it part of my own. At that moment I had no idea just how much my next case would test this particular resolve. It's time to say hello to the extremely enigmatic Carl.

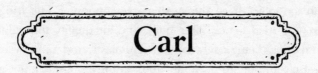

Carl

Carl was a coroner's case. He lived alone and had also died alone. Though we all die alone really, some of us just do it with people watching on. The coroner only had a name and address to give me and by the end of the call every other box on my referral form remained dolefully blank. There probably won't be any family in this case, he had surmised, and when we visited the property and stood in the same room where the coroner had been a few days before to collect the body, I understood why he had drawn this conclusion.

There was only one armchair in that living room, ironically the room where Carl had stopped doing that very same thing. Nowhere at all for family, friends or visitors to sit. He clearly didn't anticipate, or perhaps even want, any company. But backing out of the living room for a moment, let's take this from the top.

The case came in during a heatwave and our olde-worlde

non-air-conditioned office was sweltering. People had brought in desk fans but they were powerless to help and just
moved the hot air back and forth. We had a fridge freezer in
the store cupboard, the latter part of which was now stuffed
with ice lollies from the supermarket opposite. The fridge
part was used for samples, bugs, and air quality tubes, but
those things being safely contained in plastic and tupperware,
it wasn't unusual to see a lunchbox sitting alongside a pot of
lab-bound unidentified insects. You couldn't afford to be too
squeamish in this line of work. And speaking of, Steve and I
went into that same cupboard, fetched the gear, grabbed an
ice lolly each and headed off to a house where a body had lain
undiscovered in unbearable temperatures for a few weeks.

The entrance to the property, a charming little four
bedroom cottage with none of the symbolic disrepair
of Robert's place, was through a side door which took us
through a garage and into the kitchen. I instantly regretted
not wearing a full haz suit as I brushed past a motorcycle
with a cover on it which deposited a thick black patch of dirt
all down my side. As we opened the door to the kitchen the
familiar smell drifted out to greet us, though amazingly, given
the weather, not quite as strong as before. Evidently, they
had found Carl slightly more quickly than they had Robert.
There was, however, an undertone of something else which
overpowered the sweetness of the death smell and made it
more acrid. I really wasn't looking forward to discovering
what that something was.

We opened the kitchen windows to release the smell, swap
the stale hot air for fresh hot air and also free the flies that

were buzzing around. We then cracked open the anti-bacterial wipes to clear away the maggots on the sideboard which were spawning them. The first order of business, as there were already pests, was to clear away the food waste and empty the fridge. As I cleaned, I looked out of the window behind the sink and noticed a quaint cottage garden. It was stepped with a vegetable patch at the front and a couple of flowerbeds rising up behind. A hose was lying on the ground along with some tools. He had been out there quite recently. It was uplifting to get a real glimpse of his daily life, caught in a freeze frame, but also arresting, as it represented time having stopped for him forever.

Luckily I had brought my own black bags as Carl's kitchen bin was full to overflowing with ready-meal-for-one packets. Possibly evidence that he had been too ill to cook at the end, though more than likely it was just stereotypical business as usual for a single bloke living alone. The dining table was covered in boxes, post and papers, clearly not used for its intended purpose and certainly not used for family meals or to entertain.

Kitchen cleaned, we started our recce and wandered through into a small hall with a bathroom and a cupboard door coming off of it. The cupboard, to our surprise, contained some shotguns, most likely for countryside pursuits rather than terrible murders, but they couldn't stay there unattended, so Steve put in a call to the police who confirmed Carl was licensed and arranged to come and collect them from us. The hall also contained two buckets of excrement; mystery undertone solved, but the new mystery of why they were there opened up. We then very quickly pressed on to the living room and here we are, back at his armchair.

It was well worn with foam poking out through numerous holes and a tartan blanket draped over it like a second skin to extend its use. This was clearly where he spent most of his time, so why wouldn't he upgrade to a more comfortable model? He had a nice house full of quite expensive items, so Carl could clearly have afforded a replacement if he had wanted one. He must have been as attached to it as Frasier Crane's dad was to his unsightly recliner. Perhaps it had sentimental value? Could his mum or dad have occupied this chair in another life?

I could easily picture Carl wiling away many hours in this spot. It was set next to a grand open fireplace, a stack of magazines on one side, a stack of books on the other, a TV out in front. A triumvirate of solo distractions. There was an electric guitar on the floor next to the TV – which Steve remarked upon as being a very good make, being a muso himself – and a music system on the other side of the room with lots of rock and blues albums in the cabinet underneath.

Taking in the scene properly, we agreed that the whole set-up looked more like voluntary solitude rather than evidence of a lonely soul. Carl clearly had a rich internal life and plenty of things to occupy him in lieu of human company. As someone who often sought solitude themselves, who had always felt at a slight disconnect, an observer rather than a direct participant in life – many aspects of which I found unappealing and odd – and whose own parents had pegged her as an odd kid likely to end up alone, I liked him already.

In addition to being where he spent most of his time, his armchair was also clearly where he spent his final moments as the, now familiar, patch of dark black staining on the floor in front of it attested. That's another thing I have learned from this job. Not having attended such scenes before and then suddenly attending two with the same staining, I wondered what it was and educated myself. Turns out when your body is in second stage decomposition your blood comes out of your nose and mouth − fun death fact, this is called the bloat stage − and of course blood turns dark black when left to soak into a carpet or bed for a couple of weeks. The dark staining is always where the head of the person was, so every room I step into I can see where the person had been just before the coroner did their thing, thanks to nature's equivalent of the chalk outline around the body. Not a skill I can do much with, admittedly.

I threw open the window to let in some more of that hot outside air and as I forced up the stiff wooden sash, cars whizzed past outside as they had been doing for the weeks he had lain there, along with numerous pedestrians who had only been two metres from the body as they passed by. I stood there looking out of the window, at the row of shops opposite, at the pub next door, the church diagonally across the way. He lived at the top of the high street in a large town and had somehow died completely unnoticed. I tried to hold on to the fact that he didn't care for company in life so perhaps wouldn't have regarded this as particularly tragic.

Whilst I was glad he had expired in most likely his favourite spot at home, it was a shame to see the apparent manner of his passing unfolding in front of us. The sheer number of diarrhoea medication packages lying around signalled that the buckets of excrement were down to him being too poorly to frequently make it to the toilet by the end, and being alone he had no help either getting there or with the clean-up. I assumed he had caught a tummy bug and maybe dehydrated, but the inquest eventually concluded that he had undiagnosed bowel cancer. Poor guy had been treating a fatal illness with Imodium. Other brands are available. It must have been agony and really quite scary at the end. He hadn't sought medical advice until the days before he died when he phoned the doctor and asked for a call back. They phoned the next day, he didn't answer, he died shortly thereafter.

The same day that Carl put the call in to the doctor, a local relative (spoiler alert) posted a note through the door, to let him know his favourite aunt had died. They didn't ring the bell, they knew better than that. I found out later from one of his friends (more spoilers) that he hated the sound of his doorbell and resented answering the door at all. A neighbour we'd knocked for after the house search, with me forgetting I was still sporting my crime scene shoe covers and rubber gloves, had told us she'd wanted to give Carl some wine as a thank you for him watering her garden whilst she was on holiday. She'd had enough awkward encounters in the past to know to just leave the bottle by the side entrance of his house with a note and then skulk away. This wine was still in its gift bag on the floor of his kitchen along with a big untouched box from a wine merchant that he had ordered himself. He clearly liked a tipple, but his deteriorating health had put paid to cracking open any of the latest shipment or the gifted bottle, which we returned to its purchaser.

The relative's note was still on the doormat, unopened. Carl had clearly been too ill by this point to reach his doormat or to care what was on it. I opened it and thankfully they had written their phone number at the top, as there turned out to be no address books in the house for us to go on. We put it in the evidence bag, collected up all of the other post which had accumulated there over the weeks leading up to his death and in the days since, then carried on the walk through.

The hallway led to a set of steep, crooked steps with nothing to hold onto. The precarious hike brought us to a gloomy upstairs landing with very little natural light and as my eyes re-focused, I saw an unopened Christmas present from the 1980s on the floor just beside the top step. I knew this because I recognised the exact wrapping paper from my own childhood, it featured in one of my family Christmas Day photos from when I was five. Pine needles against a red background, dotted with coloured baubles. It felt significant, like it was meant for someone who never got the chance to receive it. It was a mystery that I never did unravel, literally or figuratively. Yet more evidence of stories that would remain untold, but certainly existed. Next to the present there was a vintage vacuum cleaner, the bagged type with Hoover written vertically down the side that, again, I recognised from my childhood. Time had stood still in the upper parts of this house, probably on purpose from what I had learned at Robert's.

We went down the hall, glancing through the open doors until we reached what we took to be Carl's room, as it was the only bedroom still in obvious use. It didn't contain any clues, just his clothing, though the fact he had a single bed did strike us as relevant. 'Childhood bedroom', we both said without missing a beat and putting only a perfunctory question mark inflection at the end of the utterance, as though there was any doubt that the through line of these cases wasn't continuing here. The second bedroom was being used as storage for clothes, records and general miscellany, all piled on an unmade-up mattress. There were also some framed photos propped up along the length of the bed, which itself was set against the wall, the images facing said wall. I turned them around and they seemed like old family pictures. Why were all of his family photos facing the wall with none on display anywhere in the house? The only photo on display was in the living room; a mystery woman sitting across from the person taking the shot, presumably our man Carl, in a restaurant. It was in this bedroom that I also discovered a life-long secret of Carl's, but I'm not telling. The name change won't help much if someone who knows him picks this book up, and if he didn't want anyone to know in life, I assume the same goes in death.

The third bedroom was at once full of junk but at the same

time very well organised. It was like a museum, full of items, carefully curated. A lifetime of antiques and heirlooms – as well as an Amiga 500, which appealed to my retro gamer heart – all laid out methodically on the floor. No furniture in this room, just the family history at right angles, and yet more framed photos curiously turned to face the wall. I couldn't tell if this was due to overwhelming grief or overwhelming contempt. With none of the bedrooms providing any paperwork or clues, we left the gloom of the upstairs to start the search in earnest.

Thanks to Carl, this didn't take long. His wallet was on the kitchen sideboard and he had filed all of his relevant papers from energy bills to bank statements to house deeds in one kitchen cupboard. Which is actually what I do too, so once again, I felt a kinship with him. My nominated kitchen cupboard of death-readiness is full of folders that I previously used for my university coursework, now containing my will, my accidental death cover, my car registration, every bit of useful paperwork to do with my life, along with a supplementary 'if you're reading this then I'm dead' note which gives a full list of institutions that need to be informed, online accounts that need to be closed down, and my express wishes not to waste money on a funeral, just a direct cremation, please, or whatever is cheapest or most environmentally friendly in the future world of my death.

There was a bureau in the hallway behind one of the buckets of excrement. I attempted to move it to the bathroom but couldn't, it was heavy, the handle was slipping, and the last thing we needed was shit everywhere – a universal truth that – so I opened it and went through the paperwork with my feet planted behind the bucket and my body at a right angle over it. Thankfully there wasn't much in there of importance so I only had to adopt that uncomfortable position and hold my breath for a short time. As I stepped back and concluded we were done here, we both paused and agreed that the buckets couldn't stay there. But we couldn't flush the stuff without blocking the system, so Steve put on some grippy gloves and carefully moved them outside.

We locked up, put out the bins and returned to the office-forward-slash-oven. The fans were still blowing hot air around and everyone's energy levels were low, which was unfortunate as hot days are the most complaint laden, with everyone turning up their music or lighting a bonfire and stinking up someone's freshly-laundered sheets. Eager to get going and give myself as much chance as possible to find this apparently solitary man's people, the first thing I did when I sat down at my desk, after downing some water and painkillers, was to call the phone number on the doorstep note. This person was already bereaved so I wasn't looking forward to sending more death their way.

A very elderly gent answered who, from his fragile sounding voice, I took to be the author, and therefore the very recent widower. I announced myself. Told him I was from the council, but in a gentle voice rather than a formal tone, trying to signal that this wasn't election canvassing or a parking issue; attempting to walk that peculiar line between officialdom and humanity. I asked if he was, insert name from note, and if he knew Carl. He confirmed that he did and that he was a relative by marriage, then told me what I had already read, about his wife. I didn't let on that I had seen the note and knew about her death in case that felt too strange and intrusive. I then told him the news, which on this occasion as it would with every time to come, sounded so blunt as it came out of my mouth, even with the soft voice and gentle run-up. There really is no good way to say that someone is dead, though there's a certain relief once it's out, and the conversation can start in earnest.

He let out a deep sigh. He'd clearly had enough death for one month. His voice cracked as he asked when and how. I cringed again as I let him know that it was many weeks ago, the silent subtext of alone and undiscovered hanging in the air, and that it was still with the coroner, with all of those negative connotations too. I could hear him processing and really didn't want to hit him with my next question but I was duty bound. Would he be willing to take on the funeral arrangements? His voice tensed up. He had just paid out thousands for his wife's, he was on a fixed income, very elderly, and actually despite his sadness, he barely saw Carl from one year to the next. He kept himself to himself, he explained, worried I would think poorly of him for not being there at the end and then not making the arrangements. I assured him that there was no expectation, that family didn't always equal instant closeness, and it was not a problem, I just had to ask.

The tension eased up a notch. I explained that I would be making some more calls but if I had no success it would be a council funeral. The tension re-entered as he said, 'a pauper's?' I finally got to finish the call on a brighter note as I described what we provided, a far cry from what he had imagined, and invited him to the service.

I then geared myself back up to start all over again with another number taken from a card in a pile of recent post on the kitchen table. It wasn't a greeting card for an occasion, it was a blank one with a general news and catch-up message inside, from a woman. Whose day would I be ruining this time? Deep doleful breath, and dial.

A very elderly lady answered the phone, though more robust sounding than the previous relative, an impression helped along by her broad no nonsense Yorkshire accent. I established that she was a first cousin before once again breaking the news in my ultra-gentle voice, which once again did nothing to take any of the edge off. A shocked silence gave way to a guilty admission that she had called him in the days before he died, he had been complaining of ill health and the phone went dead. He never called back and he never picked up again. She kept repeating, 'I stopped trying', 'I should have known', 'I should have let someone know'.

This call had become unexpectedly harder than the first one as her guilt exponentially grew and she looked to me for comfort and assurance. The problem was, he was so uncommunicative that she had assumed he just wanted to be left alone. He only had a phone because she had forced the issue and paid for one to be installed. She would call him up once a month and he would say very little. It seemed that Carl didn't communicate much with anyone, but still managed to mean something to them, he must have been a good guy. As with the previous relative I asked if she would be willing to take on arrangements, but at her age, at such a geographical remove, and with limited mobility and poor health, she apologetically declined. I assured her no apology was needed, but her sense of guilt was bubbling back up again as she then told me in an anxious voice that she wasn't even sure if she could handle the journey down to attend. She even found the idea of claiming some of the considerable estate to be too burdensome. I couldn't leave the call this way, so we chatted for a bit until I was satisfied she sounded relatively calm again. I told her to just process the news and forget the logistics, now was not the time to think about them.

Not for her anyway, but it was very much the time for me. The other relative had rejected to claim on the estate as well. The stress of probate was something he was too old and tired to deal with. If there are next of kin alive the Government Treasury Solicitor won't accept the referral, but if the family refuses, then what? I looked at their frequently asked questions and there was no precedent for this scenario, obviously, because most people want money. The only slight glimmer of hope was the gentleman's son who he asked me to communicate with on his behalf about the funeral, maybe he could make the application at a push. A problem for another day, I thought, and with next of kin found but nobody to do the funeral, I made my death appointment – but not that joke again, I was well over it by now – and then started on my evidence bag.

It took me six and a half hours to close down Carl's life. I froze his bank accounts, informed his pension provider, the DWP, the council tax, the gas, the electric, the water, the phone, and then after the main stuff was dealt with I went through his wallet and cancelled his library card, his loyalty cards, I even cancelled his coach holiday to Wales that coming Christmas, the confirmation for which was also in the pile of post we'd scooped up. The coach trip seemed at odds with his personality. Someone with possible social anxiety, or who at the very least was not too fond of company would surely loathe a coach trip. Shoved in together in a small space, singing Ging Gang Goolie all the way to Wales. Maybe he wasn't the loner I thought. But then again, the chat with the neighbour and the only two people from his life I had found so far certainly seemed to speak to that. None of them had any suggestions for friends or even acquaintances that I could seek out. Everyone in his immediate family was dead, they had explained. One sister in infancy, then his parents, then his other sister in the 1990s. As his family dropped away he had stayed in the familial home, alone. I went over to Steve's desk to tell him that we had made a correct guess back there in Carl's bedroom.

As he had lived in the same town his whole life I decided to try the local church across the road from his house. According to the cousin, his father had been a bell ringer there and his mother and sister had been very involved with church life, cleaning and volunteering at events. She also mentioned the possibility of a family grave, something that would be far preferable to an anonymous council plot. I headed over the next day at lunch and arrived in the middle of a half-term event, the place teeming with children, the walls covered with tinfoil as a space theme was carried out at various craft tables. I asked one of the helpers where the priest was. They pointed at a man in a Jedi robe and fake beard. My serious conversation with this fancy dress priest, who pulled the beard down every time he went to answer a question, ranks high in my most surreal moments of the job. Unfortunately he had never met Carl and the family grave was from the early 1800s and very much closed for business.

Getting a bit desperate now, I turned to Google and got a load of generic results for the many Carls with his second name. Before giving up I decided to narrow it down by putting quote marks around his name and then adding his town, as a lifetime spent there could have left a footprint. I didn't think I would get anything other than a 192.com listing but desperate times. To my amazement, there he was. Accepting an award for best chrysanthemums. And another award for daffodil bowls. And, to quote Jean, another and another. I scrolled the articles for information about the organisers of these events. A local garden club. I was in business.

Sort of. They knew him about as well as his relatives, about as well as anyone, i.e. hardly at all. A quiet man, didn't speak, kept to himself, though again, despite barely trying with anyone he had made an impression, and everyone I spoke to was sad about his death.

One person mentioned that they had complimented a plant he had grown. He had grunted back at them, the 'conversation' stalled, then hung awkwardly in the air before being dropped, and that was the end of that. Except it wasn't, and a year later Carl presented them with one he had grown from seed, just for them. He had remembered, they said, he was really kind.

The chair of the club circulated the funeral date to all of the members and happy in the knowledge that it wouldn't be just myself and a couple of distant rellies on the day, Steve and I went back to the house one more time for completeness, as there wasn't much for the eulogy besides his enjoyment of gardening, which wouldn't fill half an hour and we also needed to find and empty his car which we were told was parked on the road somewhere nearby. Cue walking around the streets clicking the key and trying to spot lights flashing whilst getting funny looks from the locals.

During this visit I had an instinct to go through a huge pile of what looked like rubbish in a dusty corner of the living room. A leaning tower of Pisa formation of junk mail, circulars, takeaway menus and local newspapers. I was glad I did because wedged in among it all I found a greeting card from 'L' talking about the good times, the nights out, the nights in and gushing about how much she loved him. This was interesting. Perhaps she was the woman in the photo. The one in the restaurant, smiling broadly, head to one side, holding up a glass to say cheers to the photographer. Maybe on one of the nights out mentioned in the card. The best part, there was an address written in there.

When I got back to the office, I looked up the phone number associated with it and dialled with my heart racing and job-share woman number two, aka Ali, watching with her hands clasped together in excitement and nervous anticipation as the story of Carl swept her along too. I was so glad to be about to speak to someone who wouldn't just say 'how sad but they didn't really know him'. He clearly had layers and his funeral was the last chance to peel them back and tell his full story. I was also less than happy to be the one to tell her that he had died. I was about to be even more unhappy when moments later I was told by the new tenant that this woman had moved away a long time ago.

Ali's face fell as I repeated the sentence out loud so she knew what was going on in the call. I Googled her hoping to have the same luck as I did with Carl himself, but to no avail. I was fairly bereft, we both were. Then just before I left for the day, the phone rang. It was another garden club member who had just heard the news and wanted to know more. They explained that they knew nothing much about Carl for the customary reasons. It being the end of the day and of my tether, I confided in them that I was hitting that problem a lot and explained my frustrating near-eureka moment with the affectionate card.

'Oh, I tell you who that might be, he used to go out with my friend's daughter Lorna, his only ever girlfriend I think. I'll get her to ring you tomorrow.'

L for Lorna, this had to be my woman. A quick high five and goodnight with Ali and I went home that evening, desperate to return to work the next morning, not a feeling I was familiar with in my previous jobs.

And there it was the next day, the red voicemail light on my phone. It was difficult listening to her message in the buzz of an open-plan office both literally, as I had to place a hand over my ear to block out a licensing officer shouting at a badly-behaved taxi driver who was arguing with her decision to give him penalty points, and also emotionally. The contrast of everyday life continuing apace against her tangible shock, her voice cracking throughout. You could hear her processing the information as she talked. It choked me up and I was grateful for this dry run where I didn't need to say anything, as I was sure I would have cried myself if we were talking in real time. She had adored him, she couldn't believe he was gone from the world, she desperately needed to know more about this unexpected death of a man who had always been as strong as an ox. She said that talking to the answering machine was therapeutic, indeed she left me numerous overnight messages during the case where she shed more light on Carl whilst talking through her own grief.

As I put the phone down and picked it straight back up to return the call, I relayed the message to Ali who was just returning with some tea. She sat down and opened the morning's post with half an eye on me as I dialled with some trepidation, but also much anticipation of finally learning about this mysterious man.

I was not disappointed. She knew everything about him. He was a gardener, a bricklayer, he'd helped to build an opera house in the area. He was a tug-of-war tugger, he loved the arts, he would go up to London alone to lose himself in the galleries, or watch a West End show. He would meet her for dinner afterwards, he loved eating out. She met him when she was younger and he used to take her for rides on his motorbike. He got her back into bikes, she wanted to buy the one he had in his garage, the one I'd rubbed up against, if that was possible. She was too old and ill to ride it anymore, but she just wanted a part of him and of their time together. He had encouraged her to travel and see the sights. He used to disappear on trips all the time. The Christmas coach trip was his annual getaway to a new place that concurrently stopped him being at home with no family on such a difficult day.

Crucially, she revealed why he was so withdrawn. His father, mother and sister had all been deaf and mute, the term used at the time, and he grew up in a silent house. Everything fell into place. He didn't speak much and hated noise because he wasn't used to it. Silence was his baseline. He was no oddball recluse. He had all of these interests and passions that connected him to the world around him, but he just didn't talk about any of them. I suddenly had the full picture of Carl, which I shared with a rapt Ali, and the rest of the office who had started to listen in, such is the power of a good story. I was now able to provide Martin with a wealth of much-needed information just in time for the funeral.

On the day Steve and I arrived to find a large group of people congregating outside the chapel, some were family, some neighbours, the majority were the garden club and fellow allotment owners. There was a buzz of activity as flowers were fetched from cars and arranged on the wall outside, and a card was circulated that everyone was signing to go on his coffin. I went over to photograph the flowers for Lorna, who couldn't be there due to ill health, and saw that one bunch was from her, with a fairly heart-breaking card attached. Another was from his distant family and another from the garden club, who had used their collective skills to bypass the florist and create a huge spray from their own flowers. A final bunch with no card turned out to be Carl's own allotment flowers that he was growing for that year's competition. You can't win them all, Carl. His fellow allotment owners had ensured they had been watered daily throughout the heatwave so that they survived and could join him at the end. Something I found far more touching than any of the expensive generic funeral bouquets I regularly saw littering the garden of remembrance on a regular basis. Proof that this category of funeral was not lower status and could actually be elevated above the ordinary by these unique moments.

The service was standing room only – a huge turnaround from my initial low expectations in that one-chair living room – so Steve and I perched on the empty organist's chair at the back to watch on. Woody Guthrie's 'Will You Miss me When I'm Gone?' played us in. A track both lifted from Carl's music collection and also eminently funeral suitable. For the reading Martin chose 'Happy the Man' by John Dryden, a poem contemplating the metaphysics of happiness. Perfect for Carl whose life could have been viewed as a sad one from an outside or conventional point of view, but was largely as he wished it. He may have been curtailed by his inability to communicate but this became a part of his character and subsequently, his wishes.

As I sat there listening to the eulogy, it struck me that the manner of his life matched the manner of his death. He would have preferred to die than be in hospital for weeks receiving treatment, or have visiting nurses coming into his home, breaking the silence and fussing over him. Lorna confirmed my thoughts in one of our phone calls, saying that she was always worried about how he would cope with needing more help and intrusions as he got older, but that problem was now solved for him, and this relief on his behalf gave her some comfort.

As Martin walked us through his life story, I watched as the garden club and even the extended family were visibly amazed to learn all about this dark horse. Looking around the room at people's eyes widening, smiles forming, heads shaking in disbelief, I felt that same feeling I had at Jean's funeral; the power of the job to bring the person back to life in the room one last time.

Some expressed regret to me afterwards that they never got to hear any of this from the man himself, but as Lorna had told me, it took many months of sitting in silence with Carl before you even got a scrap of chat. She persevered through the awkwardness because she knew there was something more going on under there. Even though it didn't last, they had made a strong bond and stayed in touch when she left town. He had even visited her at her marital home, fixed up her son's motorbike and helped to build her a patio. I didn't pry as to the reasons for the relationship ending, but from the house search it was a safe guess that he was held there in the family home, or at least the shadow of it, unable to let go. His need for silence and solitude had also clearly won out too.

Nobody cried during the service, except me obviously. I had been fully immersed in Carl, discovering him for myself, rediscovering him for others. I was also still very early on in developing my emotional balancing act.

The lack of high emotion was something Martin had anticipated and openly acknowledged in the eulogy. He had done the same for Jean's service too and probably many other public health funerals before that, where the mourners are not of the traditional sort, saying: 'Even though you may not have been especially close to him, you have still been touched by Carl's passing, and the compassion that you feel for him now, though perhaps not as strong or as deep as love, is still a mark of the fact that Carl's life, and his presence in this world, mattered.'

This truth was borne out when after the service, a woman from the allotment approached me and said 'I used to wave at Carl when I went down there, and yesterday I looked over and he wasn't there, and it actually made me so sad I cried.' It was nice to see him mourned in his own unique Carl way. Then, as everyone drifted off, Martin walked over for a debrief and a chat. His parting words as he walked towards his car were: 'Your funerals are never ordinary, I can't wait to see what comes next.' Nor could I.

When I got back to the office with my now traditional puffy eyes, I switched gears and tackled the grounding inbox of doom and bins, trying to work out what to say to a random complaint about a neighbour's Christmas lights going up too early. I developed the pictures of the flowers and the coffin in my lunch hour and posted them first-class recorded to Lorna so that she didn't feel too far removed from the day. At my own expense, so again, at ease taxpayer.

Then over the coming days I was relieved to learn that the son of Carl's favourite aunt wanted to claim the estate for the family, saving me a big government referral job.

I met him at the house to sign over the keys and my paper trail. He hadn't been inside the place since childhood, Carl didn't accept guests, so we did a walk around together where he took in the scene and pieced his relative together in much the same way as I had on day one. He had a big job ahead, cleaning the place up and clearing it out, and looked shell shocked as we returned to the kitchen for the sign-over. He was visibly relieved when I handed him a neat bundle of papers and bills, annotated with dates of freezing or closure, reference numbers, a breakdown of all the refunds paid back into Carl's estate; at least he didn't also need to listen to several hours of tedious hold music.

When the case was closed I had a phone call from Lorna. She wanted to say thanks for the photos. She also hesitantly asked if I had come across Carl's secret. I confirmed that I had. It was something that only she had ever been party to. The job once again bringing me into people's private worlds, starting out as officialdom and ending in intimacy. She also wanted to thank me on behalf of Carl. I managed a whispered 'you're welcome' before my voice cracked and tailed off. She could hear I was wobbling and she was clearly about to cry too, so we both said goodbye before it became too difficult, and weird. Her last words were 'just thank you, from a friend' before the phone went dead for the final time.

I sat there in a bleary-eyed daze and was then instantly brought back to earth as I often am, by a complaint call. Someone annoyed that their neighbour was shouting loud sweary abuse at their Amazon Alexa. A blunt reminder that the absurd business of life goes relentlessly on irrespective of loss and of pain and of the implosion of individual worlds. To this day, I still go back and forth over whether that is a comforting fact or not.

There was however a good deal of comfort to be derived from the redemptive power of the job I was now becoming thoroughly immersed in. The transformative impact of those extra efforts, the Google search, that last look in the pile of junk paper, they had opened up an entire life that would otherwise have remained obscured.

I had told someone's story, kept their secret, felt a connection and, as Martin had observed, this opportunity to raise the funeral above and beyond the basic and the ordinary would be waiting for me time and again. But my next case though would be less about getting to know my referral, and more about getting her where she needed to be. Introducing, Angela.

Angela

My car had been very close to a write-off, but not close enough, and so two months, two funeral cases, and three and a half thousand pounds of repair work later, I got it back. I wasn't entirely sure how I felt about this. I had bought it new just a year before the crash and whilst I didn't doubt the workmanship, it didn't really feel like a new car anymore. The idea of having the whole of the front destroyed and then replaced made it feel like I was just driving around in a legalised cut and shut. But not wanting to stay in the doldrums any longer, I counted my blessings; fixed-up motor, fixed-up me – courtesy of a course of physio – and a compensation pay out that cleared the never-never sofa debt. Things were back on track.

Two weeks after the fix I drove to London for a birthday party and parked in the underground car park of a Mayfair hotel, thinking that would mean safety for my humble Micra amongst the Porsches and Maseratis of the metropolitan elite. It didn't. The place was a magnet for criminals looking to rob rich people, of which I am not one – I wasn't staying at the posh hotel, I was paying twenty quid to park underneath it – but they had to completely smash out my back window and steal my overnight bag with some knickers, a phone charger and a toothbrush in it to find that out. And despite me doing that thing where you look back at the car when you leave it – as though to secure it further with the power of positive thought.

When I returned to the car after the party I could see something was up. The light on the wall, which had filled the car with a glow as I had walked away after parking up, was now interrupted by something. This something turned out to be the parcel shelf – I didn't know it was called that until I had to look it up to describe it just now, every day's a school day – which had been pulled and twisted right up.

As I quickened my steps I saw glass shards all over the floor and a gaping hole where the rear windscreen had once been. Someone had broken the window and pulled the – time to use that term again for the second and probably final time of my life – parcel shelf up to see what treasures my boot held. Their inevitable disappointment was my only comfort. The car park 'attendant' who hadn't been there when I arrived evidently wasn't there when it happened, and wasn't there now (so maybe needed a new job title). He had stuck a note to my driver's door with a police reference number on it.

I put it in my bag and then just stood there. I didn't know what to do next. Did I just drive off now? Was it even legal to drive with no back windscreen? I had to decide fast as my parking permit was up in ten minutes' time. At the stroke of midnight my ticket would turn into a pumpkin and if I was still stood there gawking at something that wasn't improving for being stared at, I would owe the owners twenty more pounds.

My brain ran the scenarios. I was two hours from home and already looking at a two-in-the-morning bedtime as it was. If I called a twenty-four hour repair or recovery person I would have to wait in an underground car park next to the scene of a crime, where I could possibly get bonus robbed in person just to complete the night. I would also be legally robbed by the out-of-hours charges plus the extra car park fees. And I might not see my bed until well into the next day. Five minutes left to decide, tick tock. Executive panicky decision made, I smashed out the rest of the window as far as I could, exited the car park with two minutes left on my ticket and drove all the way to the coast with the wind blowing in my hair, pretending I was in a convertible, and hoping nobody pulled me over. All the way I tried to remain positive and keep the ever-creeping persecution complex at bay.

I thought about how it wasn't the worst thing that had ever happened to anyone at that hotel. Alexander Litvinenko has been poisoned there a few years earlier, there's always someone more badly off than you. I then decided to take the line that it could have been worse, the car could have been stolen rather than trashed and ransacked. Small mercies.

I also threw in a bit of guilty liberal sympathy for the crim. They probably had a terrible life, whereas I had a nice job and a comfy home to take my bashed-in car back to. It was I who should feel sorry for them really. Ya da, ya da.

After the kind of uneasy night's sleep you tend to have when there is some looming task coming up the next day, I called out a windscreen repair company first thing in the morning and watched a very uncertain young man do what looked like a very bad job. Firstly, smashing the remaining solid glass onto my back seat and driveway, then yanking the spoiler off after it wouldn't unhook, and finally fitting the new glass with lumps of unsightly glue all around the edges. He said not to touch the car for a week, which I dutifully did, or rather didn't.

Then a week later I went out to put something in the boot. When I closed it again, a bit of the spoiler fell off. This minor incident compared to all that went before was just petty enough to provide the final straw and I stood there and had a good cry. The one I should have just gone ahead and had in the first place. I felt much better for it. It was extremely unfair that just after getting the front fixed I then had to get the back fixed. It was extremely unfair that neither thing had been my fault. And however down on their luck they were, screw them for doing that to me, who had done nothing to them. There is a time and a place for being philosophical and counting your blessings and that time is not in the immediate aftermath of someone robbing you.

Thankfully the company came back out, fixed the spoiler, replaced the replacement glass which they confirmed the guy had fitted completely wrong and then gave me half my money back too. The therapeutic cry and the slight upturn in my luck signalled the start of a proper return to form. In the weeks and months that followed there were no more major events, just the normal acceptable nuisances of everyday life, and I was able to finally focus on normal daily living rather than the administrative aftermath of minor emergencies. The final pieces of furniture were bought and I finally felt at home in the new life I had come down to escape to.

Back at work the cases continued to roll in and next up was Angela, who didn't actually end up having a council funeral, and who only took me a matter of days to conclude, but the amount of effort compressed into this timescale was worthy of any of my full-term assignments, so she gets an honorary mention, both for that and for toughening me up in the process. Each case, I was starting to learn, teaches you something new, and brings something more out of you.

She was called in on a Wednesday. I only remember this because Dave in the corner was, in between phone calls, practising his questions on us for the pub quiz he was hosting that night. He even emailed everyone the picture round at one point. The call came from a solicitor who was presiding over her estate, which they immediately pointed out was already deeply in debt to the care home she had died in, as well as numerous other creditors, including themselves. They were never going to see their own fee, they grumbled, especially as a council funeral would have first call on the estate and trump them in the pecking order. Well, hello to you too.

Once they had bemoaned their lot, at length, we got down to the task in hand. Angela was a widow who had been estranged from her two daughters for coming on forty years now. The solicitor gave me their contact details with a huge side of 'for what it's worth' as they wearily pointed out that neither one had ever replied to any correspondence or accepted a call relating to their mother. I initially found the solicitor's attitude frustratingly gloomy and hard work. Little did I know that I would be right there with them within a matter of days.

There was one other relative they remarked, a niece, who had arranged the funeral of Angela's husband a few years prior. The daughters had no time for either parent it seemed. You don't get a rift that significant and deep over a mere trifle though. I wondered who had severely wronged who. Maybe I would find out from the niece, my only positive lead. Even if she didn't want to take on a second funeral – which would be perfectly understandable, being tapped up twice in the absence of those customarily responsible is a pretty big ask – she might at least want to attend.

I then took the care home details and started my calls. The easy one first, to the care home to arrange a time to visit. Then the niece, who turned out to be the wife of a sitting Lord. He was the one who picked up my call in fact, which made it a lot easier, as he was at a slight remove and extremely formal, a far cry from the calls I had made to Carl's family. The Lord didn't pass me to his wife, whom he described as being too emotionally unstable to deal with any more of this family's issues. The solicitor and now the niece; seemed like anxiety and ennui were contagious with this case. I mentioned the daughters, how they had both declined to take my calls, hanging straight up, and palpable tension entered his voice as he informed me that they didn't even bury their father, he and his wife had to, and weren't very happy about being asked a second time. This was my first experience of a case of family breakdown and estrangement and my heart sank a little as I listened to him rant and waited for him to decline, realising that once he did, I would have a very hard time magicking this one up a happy ending.

Thankfully, as much as he baulked at having to do it again, he baulked even harder at the idea of a council funeral for his aunt by marriage. Her strict Jewish faith demanded certain rites and requirements, which I confirmed the council could not entirely stretch to, and so, faced with the stark choice of a shared council plot or a specific blessed grave in the Jewish section of the cemetery next to her husband, he agreed to take the funeral off my hands.

As I hung up someone shouted 'Erinsborough' across the room, presumably in answer to a question Dave had set about Neighbours, and my mood lifted a little as I sent a confirmatory email of our conversation, cc the solicitor, who could presumably knock off that evening happy in the knowledge that my costs were off the table, and then went home for the day myself, pleased to have diverted Angela back towards a family funeral. It was as close to a happy conclusion as I could conjure.

The next morning I arrived in the office and met Dave on the stairs. There would be no more pop quizzes today as he was heading over to the town hall to count postal votes. When he returned at lunchtime he would tell us how someone had literally spoiled their ballot by wiping their arse on it before sending it back. Quite the political statement, or possibly a vote for (insert party you don't like here to complete joke).

As he went off for this fun with democracy, I got to my desk and logged on. My heart sank as I saw the reply to my previous night's email.

My simple question about gaining consent to register the death on behalf of the family (because it has to be done within five days and we were on day four) had seemingly opened up a crack in the door which the Lord, having slept on it, had stuck his size nine right into. The gist of the message was, we're going on holiday next week, so yes please do register the death, and while you're at it, you may as well do the whole thing. The wording, 'may as well', was particularly grim. Usually reserved for banal situations like the offer of a cup of tea that you weren't particularly craving, but if you're putting the kettle on anyway. He also tacked on a peculiar line of justification about Angela having paid her rates, so bring on the council funeral. Yes, for a monthly fee we, amongst other things, collect your bins and then one day collect and dispose of you too. I mean, we do, but it's usually the last resort, not an alternative over fifties' life cover plan, and certainly nobody's ideal.

I sat there and tried to square this casual brush-off with the seemingly sincere tones of the person I had spoken to the day before, who had been talking about his conscience demanding things be done properly; the rites, the rituals, the grave plot. Though the underlying frustration and weariness were there so I suppose it wasn't a great shock. I phoned him up, figuring email always sounds hard and blunt, and that spoken interaction might get us back on track. Nope. He repeated the sentiments of his message, his voice no longer tense, now nonchalant. He was in holiday mode, I figured, he certainly kept mentioning it. A month-long trip for his wedding anniversary which they were departing for in a few days and that this was threatening to overshadow. I could understand that completely, this wasn't a close relative and they had already dealt with one funeral on behalf of the absent daughters. However, as he started to throw demands at me for what he wanted the council funeral to look like upon his return one month hence, I realised the starkness of the choice I had presented to him the day before hadn't actually landed, or maybe it had, but he perhaps thought, especially given his position in life, that he could just get what he wanted with a little bit of pressure. I would need to hot-house an air of authority for this case.

He wanted me to buy the plot next to her husband and phone a specific Jewish funeral director to oversee the service. Time to deploy that faux authority that would hopefully become real if I believed hard enough. I explained that whilst we honoured religious beliefs as far as we could – insofar as we did not burn those of, say, a Jewish or Muslim faith and did not bury those who followed for example Hinduism, and that we would always ensure that a representative of the faith took the ceremony and carried out the rites – these extra, very specific requests were more characteristic of a private funeral and fell outside of our remit. We aren't a high street funeral directors with catalogues to flick through, we're a public body and as such we have to treat every case the same, hence our written procedures and fixed contracts with a funeral home. I told him that I had never been put in this position before, not least because I was wet behind the ears and totally new to all this, but I kept that quiet, saying instead that this was because council funerals didn't usually have express wishes attached to them as there is typically nobody around to make them and even if there is, they would be too humble to demand them.

Ultimately though, not really knowing enough yet, I told him I would have to go away and find out if this was something we could avail, but with the honking great caveat that we almost definitely couldn't.

In the meantime, I had to drop in at Angela's former care home to search through her things and seek out anyone who had known her. The Lord and niece had not been in her life very much. If I ended up doing this funeral I needed material. I hitched a lift with Jon, an officer who was doing a job in the area that morning. We went to look at the site of one of his planning appraisals, stared at a field for a bit, and then headed onwards to the home.

The search of her room lasted mere minutes. A few dresses, an empty handbag and a handful of photographs. Holiday snaps, seemingly from around the time when the Costas were taking off in popularity. They were of what I took to be the two daughters, as well as Angela in giant early 1970s sunglasses, and presumably her late husband, having dinner outdoors at a resort, lounging by a pool, sightseeing, swimming. Knowing the timelines, it was more than likely one of the last occasions that they were all together. Whatever had split the family, it was clear that the photos were treasured possessions.

Her only possessions in fact, possibly symbolising a huge weight of life-long regret. I took the photos and picked out a dress for her to be buried in. The remainder would go to the charity shop and the room would probably be someone else's by the weekend. It was an object lesson in the fleeting nature of life. Her wedding ring was taken out of the care home safe and handed to me along with her wedding photos. The stunning young woman in the pictures looked so thoroughly happy. Thankfully she had no idea how it would all end and was frozen in time forever, enjoying that moment.

We sat down with a nurse who was attempting to feed a half-asleep resident in the day room to ask if she knew Angela or if she had any friends we could speak with. Sadly not. Like many in her wing, she had advanced dementia and didn't mix much. She would often become distressed and scream out her deceased husband's name. She hadn't attended his funeral due to ill health and it had haunted her to the end. Zoinks, this case just kept getting darker.

As we drove back to the office, the sad image of a woman tormented by the split in her family and the loss of that last goodbye with her husband, now being denied the poetic closure of getting buried beside him, played on my mind. I racked my brains for ways to convince the family to take back the funeral. I had spoken to my bosses and even phoned the head of the Institute of Cemetery and Crematorium Management to ask about how far our honouring of religious requirements stretched, and they confirmed what I really already knew; certainly not as far as buying a £1,780 private grave plot with £1,830 of interment fees on top. Even if it could be claimed back from the estate, we had to treat everyone equally.

They also echoed my own sentiments about the requests being akin to a private funeral purchase, rather than an appeal to a council crisis service. Grey area done away with, I was on a solid footing with which to return to the family and push things over the line. The council funeral would place her in a shared plot on the opposite side of the graveyard to where her husband was buried. Only her family could buy the plot beside him and give her the – admittedly saddest ever – happy ending. As we sat in traffic, I flicked through her wedding photos and silently promised young Angela that I would try and get her there.

When we got back I heard about the dirty protest ballot, baulked, then laughed, then baulked again, and then fired off a quick email to the solicitor asking if they knew anything about Angela for the eulogy that I might still need to contribute towards, desperate times and all that, and then phoned the Jewish funeral director that the Lord had requested.

I knew right off the bat that he was going to be an excellent ally. He had spoken to the Lord initially, when the family were set to organise things, and was therefore quite shocked to hear from me out of the blue. The Lord had gone on holiday and evidently not told him about the change of hands. He was even more shocked to hear that Angela was to remain in the mortuary for a whole month whilst the family holiday played out. Jewish tradition dictates a quick burial, ideally twenty-four hours after death, something that had been unsettling me the whole time I had been dealing with her case. Whilst that ship had already admittedly sailed, it would be halfway around the world by the time she was finally buried. The poor woman would be spinning in her grave if she could only ever get into it.

I explained the so-near-yet-so-far grave situation and my aim to get the family back on board. He got straight on Team Angela with me and said that he would phone the Lord right away and appeal to his sense of duty. His passion gave me some confidence that he would get his way and I was relieved to have someone with his zeal and authority fighting Angela's corner with me. He also offered to perform the service for free if it ended up as a council funeral and provide pall bearers from his synagogue. I was grateful to have some sort of consolation prize for her in that unfortunate event. She would at least get the full, dignified works.

Once he rang off to start persuading the Lord, I checked my emails and the reply from the solicitor was in. The person who had called in the referral hadn't known her very well, but they had found a partner who had been in her long-term employ. The headlines from her were: she loved music, dancing, theatre and old movies. She had lived in America for a while and met Clark Gable on a film set. She had a passion for shoes and loved the colour red. She adored her husband and spoke with great sadness and distress at the estrangement of her two daughters, which she said was due to herself and her husband disapproving of their choice of partners.

I read it out to Ali and we surmised from the length, and therefore the implied seriousness of the rift, that the girls must have married outside of their religion. If so, how horribly ironic that Angela's funeral, which might in another, happier universe have been organised within the customary twenty-four hours by her daughters, had now fallen well outside of her religion's bounds because of her stringent adherence having alienated them. We may have been wrong, most of these cases involved viewing snippets of facts as though in a dark room with a faulty flashlight, but the job had developed my nose for a clue, and it seemed to fit. Other people in the office chipped in to suggest that she may just have been a not very nice person. Maybe so, maybe not, it didn't matter now, death is a great leveller, and my job was to tie things up judgement-free and secure her a decent ending.

I came in the next day and sat at a hot desk next to the elections team who were busy fielding calls, one of which was a complaint from a resident about being sent the wrong postal ballot; Boris Johnson wasn't on there as an option. They tried to explain several times that you vote for the local MP of the party you support, but from their repeated explanations, each wearier than the last, and the eventual abrupt click of the receiver at the other end, I assumed it didn't land and another poo-covered ballot would be winging its way to poor old Dave.

Then my own phone rang with some good news from my ally. The Lord was back on board the funeral bus and was willing to buy the grave plot. We'd done it. However, before I got a chance to high five myself I heard a 'but'. How very characteristic of this case, which always seemed to be one step forward and two steps back. The cemetery needed a signature for the grave purchase, which should have been easy, but they only accepted the signature of the person buying the grave. The person who was abroad for a month. They didn't accept representatives or e-signatures, which the Lord had been happy to send across via his secretary. This had irritated him and he was considering walking away again.

I asked the funeral director to leave it with me and immediately picked up the phone to the cemetery, knowing that this sticking point was just waiting to be seized upon by this very changeable chap, whether calculatedly or out of exasperation at how difficult things were becoming, thus landing Angela back at my door and crucially away from her husband.

As before, I painted the picture of a sparse council burial, played up the husband angle and put on my best begging voice, but the guy was a brick wall. It had to be done this way, it was always done this way, these are the rules and there is no way around them. We went back and forth a number of times and eventually, as I was holding my head with my non-phone hand, eyes covered in despair, square one calling me and Angela right back to it, I spontaneously exclaimed 'Maaaaaaaaate, come on, there MUST be a workaround, there's ALWAYS a workaround.' There was a pause. I don't think either of us, or anyone in the open plan around me, were expecting that. Then out of the silence came the sound of him thinking followed by: 'Weeeeeeell, you could always ask the synagogue to sign it, they own it, they could buy it and transfer it.' Just imagine if I had given up after the sixth 'there's definitely no way'.

Brimming with pride at another excellent save, and starting to go from faux to actual confidence like a death admin version of Pinocchio becoming a real boy, I got back on the phone to the funeral director who was equally delighted at this news and rang right off to tell the Lord. Whilst he was doing that, I had one last hurdle to jump. The synagogue had to agree to make the purchase for a non-member.

After the battle of wills I'd just had with the cemetery bloke I was unprepared for them to immediately agree after only one rendition of my now well-worn tragic ballad of Angela. Well that was easy, I thought. Too easy, as it turned out. Enter sticking point number two; they required ten years of back synagogue fees. An annual payment that's part funeral plan, part contribution to the staff and upkeep. Angela wasn't a member and if she wanted to gain equal status with those who had been paying their monthly subs, it would be around £6,000 to get level. In the made-for-TV version of this book, I would at this point be doing a very weary look down the barrel of the camera.

Half delighted at securing the plot, not once but twice, and half dreading the Lord's inevitable backlash, I emailed all parties – Lord, funeral director, synagogue and cemetery – confirming the situation. I did so in a deliberately breezy tone and signed off with a sense of marked finality, wishing them all the best for the funeral and the future, goodbye. It was a mixture of a Jedi mind trick – this is great, you are pleased about this, yes you are – and jinx times infinity, no returns. The fact that everyone was copied in, and therefore seen to be watching, would also hopefully seal the deal. I then went to lunch and treated myself to a Virgin Pina Colada slushie on the beach for all of this hard work that I didn't even have to do because I was basically helping a family organise their own private burial on top of my actual workload out of pure respect for the deceased. And yes, I purposefully omitted to use any punctuation in that last sentence because that's how I was actually talking by this point.

I had a hunch that I would return to the email that was indeed waiting for me, and would regret opting for the Virgin Pina Colada as I opened and read the inevitable. The Lord took serious exception to the synagogue fees – I couldn't blame him, after he had just got used to the idea of buying the plot and paying for the interment, he was now being hit up for a hefty six grand on top, but them's the rules – and he customarily threatened to walk away completely unless he was offered a 'reasonable solution from one of you'.

At this point my ever-eclectic workload had me going to a meeting about new IT software, so I took my laptop along and sat there doing my usual trick of pretending to type notes about the meeting when I was actually also doing my emails. The trick is to type and pause in line with what is being said in the room. Wait for a salient point, nod whilst pulling a face that says 'Hmm, interesting' and then resume typing so it looks like you're transcribing it. Good, right? You are most welcome. And so, in this manner, I sat there and composed my final, final email, with the ghost of Angela standing over my shoulder pushing me on.

The solution, I wrote, was as before, as it had always been, and would always be. A simple choice. Pay for the private family funeral or don't pay for the disposal of remains under public health law. Bury Angela next to her husband in a blessed grave, or place her in a shared grave away from him. I paused in line with the meeting, waited, nodded meaningfully, and resumed typing. The council remit was fixed, the private fees were fixed. There was no golden combination of private funeral carried out by public body. Another pause, earnest face, and continue.

I then went ahead and made the decision for him, writing that as willingness had been demonstrated several times, with the only objection being to specific obstacles and costs imposed by the private burial of choice, I no longer considered this case eligible under Section 46 – oh yes, deliberate use of the formal description in legislation there as I tried to sound authoritative in the face of a Lord, I had truly hot-housed that status at last – and I announced that I had duly closed the case. I then took two biscuits from the plate in the middle of the table as I had more than earned them.

It was a total bluff, the case was very much still sitting there poised in my workload, and the statutory duty absolutely remained if he actually went ahead and called it, but it was worth a go. I knew that this was a wealthy family, I had Googled them, seen their many businesses, their mansion, so was confident it would not be a huge hardship, and ultimately I knew that taken to the brink this was the choice they would make because they made it before with her husband. So I took them to the brink, for Angela, and they made the right choice.

The burial took place the next week. The family gave the funeral director permission to go ahead without them, as he did not think it proper that she remained in a mortuary for that long beyond religious tradition, and on reflection they tended to agree. In return, he extended them the offer he had made me and performed the service for free. His kindness is open ended, as he has since made me that offer for another referral I had and said I can call on him any time. You meet some amazing people doing this job. He even volunteered his time to coach a family on performing the service themselves once when they decided to choose a civil ceremony with a nod to Judaism because their relative was Jewish with a strong emphasis on the 'ish'.

When it was all wrapped up, and I'd dropped the death certificate at the cemetery and the wedding ring and photos with the solicitor, and finally, wearily closed the case, I received this email from him: 'I just wanted to thank you and to let you know how grateful I am for all your hard work and effort in dealing with the late Angela. I am truly appreciative and know that without your input she would not have been laid to rest next to her husband. Wishing you all the very best for the future.'

Settling Angela's case at the same time as settling into my new life, those final best wishes for my future felt like the official end to a bad chapter and tacit permission to move forward without trepidation, and happy. I celebrated with an early night, if practically passing out counts as that.

She wasn't alone at the end, she had dutiful relatives and two people who cared what happened to her despite never having known her. In addition to leaving me feeling semi-heartened, her case had also solidified my confidence in the job, and people. I now knew that I could hold my own, deal with all-comers and fight the corner of whoever came across my desk, and find allies to help me on my way.

It taught me that circumstances might not always be ideal, and to accept grim realities whilst still trying for the best possible outcome. This latter lesson was to come in somewhat handy for my next case, where grim realities were seemingly in abundance. Here comes dodgy Matthew.

Matthew

Months after being brought in to assist on the guidance, I found myself leading on funerals. From not being able to stomach my lunch on day one, to nonchalantly clearing up maggots with anti-bacterial wipes whilst planning that night's dinner in my head; it was quite a turnaround.

I was also suddenly the random de-facto expert on private land burials. The funeral connection in my work meaning that if someone phoned up to ask how to bury mother in the back garden, the call would be put straight through to me. I did some research on the environment agency and natural burials websites and advised as best I could. The main thing to remember if you want to do the same is not to do it near a watercourse and to ensure a good depth, as the last thing anyone needs is the dog digging them up.

I was also the go-to person to answer all of the funeral freedom of information requests, which are copious. I would often see the results pop up in news stories. X per cent of councils have a service and so on. I was glad to always be able to answer in the affirmative and end up in the good stats column. When the funeral requests came in, I no longer toddled across to an officer's desk to let them know. I rallied, organised the logistics, booked the visits, packed the gear, then roped in an available colleague for the search. Usually Steve, as even though this was my area now, I had started out with him, and there was a certain security in having my mentor along. He was also a lot of fun. Fun sounds like an inappropriate thing to be having when dealing with the dead, but the car journeys were long and the mood on site needed to be lightened. Most importantly though he had the same approach to the job as me, taking a real interest in the person and always looking out for clues to their character.

My promotion had come about in part due to ability – Cathy, as before with the writing, had spotted an aptitude and had run with it, she was really good at seeing people's strengths and pointing them in that direction – but in larger part it was due to austerity. Years of cuts were about to be topped off by our central government support grant being withdrawn, as it was for most councils, something that would leave us collectively £7.8 billion down by 2025 according to the Local Government Association. So if you were wondering why your council tax is going up all the time whilst your services are stagnant or falling away, it's because of cuts so deep that those rises are in place so that we can just about stay level. And that was before Covid-19 and Brexit torpedoed the economy.

While we're on the subject of finances, the traditional grievance that council workers hear on the phones day in, day out is a variation on the theme of 'honestly I don't know what I'm paying my extortionate council tax for'. One woman who ranted at me erroneously about a missed bin concluded with the traditional council tax lament and then added: 'All I need is my rubbish collected. I mean, I don't even use the library!' Oh to be able to candidly reply that we, the district, receive only ten per cent of your annual contribution, which has to cover environmental health, elections, parks, leisure, waste, estates, benefits, planning, licensing and housing. The rest is split between the county council, who fund schools, libraries, care, transport and roads, then the police, and finally the fire and rescue service. Quite good value, I'd say. Though she would probably have just countered that her house wasn't even on fire. Dead people are so much easier to deal with.

Needing to do more with less, it made financial sense to allow me to take on funerals instead of a higher paid officer, who could then be released to do more work elsewhere. The loophole that allowed for this was that, whilst most of our work had an element of enforcement to it, and only an officer had the right to enforce, funerals weren't imposed – I mean, burning or burying someone against their will would be more something a serial killer would do – they were willingly requested, they had just ended up in officer's laps because they came as part and parcel of public health work.

Cathy created a new job role just for me at a slightly higher pay grade, which encompassed all of the betwixt and between tasks that were higher than admin but not quite officer level.

It was a win for us both. A little bit more money for me, a lot more value for them.

The only sticking point with the promotion was that my ultimate aim, once settled into life by the sea, which I now was, was to get out there and actually live it, and for this I needed to go part time. Selling up in London and buying in a small coastal town had eradicated my mortgage. Just as well, I couldn't have afforded a mortgage on coastal town wages. With that out of the way and my shonky health, dropping a couple of days made sense. I applied for part time with some sadness, as I had just after all these years stumbled across what I felt was my vocation. I then got on with work as usual whilst waiting to hear back. Though there was nothing usual about any case, least of all this next one. Just as Jean had given me some welcome respite from the pain of a house search, Matthew gave me some even more welcome respite, from the pain of forming an emotional attachment to my case. Yes, in death as in life, you're not going to like everybody.

His case arrived first thing on a Monday morning as I was having breakfast at my desk; a healthy cereal bar, if you ignored the chocolate chips, and some fruit for balance, that I wasn't eating as, due to a serious design flaw, it didn't contain chocolate chips, so balance duly lost. I really have to stop regarding buying fruit, arranging it on my desk, then giving it to a colleague as being on a par with eating it.

Job-share woman number one, aka Tina, and I were going through the inboxes whilst she had one of my five a day for me and divvying up all of the complaints that represented people's slightly spoiled weekends. Working in environmental health has made Mondays even more intolerable and made me actually dread bank holidays. The Tuesday after a bank holiday weekend has the power of a thousand Mondays. More time for people to get on each other's nerves. That first morning back you hear about every lawnmower that was turned on at five to eight, every stereo that was turned up too loud for a couple of hours at the family barbecue, and it's our kamikaze job to tell them that being annoyed once doesn't constitute a statutory nuisance, sorry.

The first email in the environmental health box on this particular morning was entitled 'smouldering dung heap'. Welcome to Monday! The second, third and fourth were bins of course. I was quite grateful for the funeral job when it came.

A voicemail had been left by a care home manager, requesting instructions on what to do with the body of someone with no next of kin. It was good of them to ask. It costs money to move bodies about and care homes sending the deceased to any old undertaker before calling it in had become a sufficiently troublesome issue that we had ended up having to send a mail shot with our nominated funeral director's details and a warning that the fee would be bounced the home's way in future if they didn't take heed.

I phoned back on the number they had left but it cut off. So I Googled the care home and called the number on their website. This time it rang and a recorded voice gave me two options, the manager or the office. I chose 'manager'.

'Sorry, time has expired,' said a recorded voice and hung up. How very apt given the nature of my call. I phoned back and chose 'office' instead then. 'Sorry, time has expired,' I was told again. This existential answering machine seemingly wanted to ram home the point that for Matthew, it really had.

There was nothing for it, I would have to complete the referral in person. Steve wasn't around so I nabbed Catherine, a trainee officer who was leaving the next week to go travelling, so wasn't taking on any more new cases and had time to tail me.

The visit didn't take long. It transpired that he had only been with them a month or so and wasn't in residential care proper, but nursing care, palliative, for a fast-moving cancer, and still had a flat somewhere. Dang it, the easy care home with no house search case was in fact a double hit; a search not only of the care home room but also of the flat.

Upon arrival, before we tackled the room, we talked to the manager who had called it in. A friendly but harassed woman trying to run a sizeable and busy home whilst her mobile kept ringing with calls that she said she had to take – probably from people who had been told time had expired by the main switchboard line – and to make matters more stressful, room alarms were going off at regular intervals in the background, so accordingly ours was a disjointed and hurried chat.

I gradually completed the basic referral information between calls and when I had everything I needed I pushed my luck and quickly asked if he had any interests. She fished out his sparsely-populated cheat sheet and informed me that he liked classical music and was a member of a local society. I Googled them whilst she took another call and noted down the phone number. Maybe they could play at the service.

People he knew, playing the music he loved. I was really enjoying trying to fit these funerals to the individual.

'Anything else?' I enquired.

'Sorry, no,' came the answer, as her hand went up to signal another call coming in.

Fair enough, they hadn't known him very long and he had been dying the whole time, so obviously wasn't at his chattiest. Another ring, ring – 'sorry I need to take this' – later and we called time on the interview, mouthing and miming our thank yous as we packed up and backed out. As we got to the door she waved us back and thrust a piece of paper at me with contact details on. She covered the receiver and quickly explained that he had two best friends who had come to see him regularly, they had also been left half of his estate each and were nominated as co-executors of his will. There was only one number on the page, Jim's. She had called him when Matthew died but he didn't have the means to pay for a funeral.

'He's an interesting man,' she said with a raised eyebrow.

A wave of relief came over me. The detective part of the job was rewarding but stressful because of the constant fear that I would draw a blank that time around and fail my person. I could leave this poor woman be and get the rest of the detail about him from his friends, who also thankfully represented two ready-made funeral attendees, and someone to hand the flat and contents to at the end.

Needing a moment to recover from the chaos of that conversation, I stepped outside to the grounds and finished my note-taking on a bench next to some dozing old ladies.

Trying to write whilst someone spoke at the speed of light meant I wouldn't be able to read half of my scrawl in an hour's time, best to tidy it up whilst fresh in my mind. I then used the down time to call the classical music society. They had never heard of him, most odd. I wrote a question mark next to that note on my sheet and finally tried the number of 'interesting man' Jim.

She wasn't wrong. He was frenetic, bouncing from irrelevant topic to distracted musing from the off. He didn't seem very upset. Or even a bit upset. Everyone deals differently of course but then he started being jovial about something seriously unpleasant.

Halfway through our conversation he volunteered that the reason the home didn't have a number for the other executor, Richard, was because he didn't have a phone. He wasn't allowed one because he had been in prison. Apparently for looking at pictures of children,' he said, chuckling away.

For apparently read definitely. When I Google-searched the guy after the call I saw that he had been inside twice. Once for possession of several thousand images and a second time for reoffending on the images and committing an outlawed sex act. I didn't look into that any further, I was using my work phone and even if I wasn't, I didn't want to know or to end up with some seriously odd targeted ads in my browser.

This guy was one of Matthew's best friends and, according to Jim, Matthew had visited him weekly during both stretches in prison. Maybe he was just extremely naive, maybe he wasn't but turned a blind eye, which would be bad enough, or maybe he, well, ick.

I shoved down my natural human instincts and remained polished and professional.

When I mentioned Matthew's interest in classical music and the dead-end call to the society, Jim told me that he didn't know what I was talking about and that Matthew didn't like classical music at all. Maybe it was a cheat sheet mix-up, or maybe he gave it as a dummy hobby, his real hobbies not being appropriate for sharing. Of course this was salacious conjecture on my part and I tried to remain neutral about the guy, resolving to do my best for him as with everyone, but he wasn't coming out of this case looking great.

I met back up with Catherine in the foyer and we headed over to Matthew's room, which turned up very little in the way of practical items or paperwork, just a mobile phone, a wallet and an inordinate amount of soft focus photos of women with their tops off. Amateur shots, obviously his own handiwork. How this hadn't registered as an interest for his cheat sheet was a mystery. At least they were of age, I thought, but they were still kind of bleak and sleazy and Catherine, who knew nothing of the conversation I had just had with Jim, said she didn't like the feel of this guy one bit.

He'd had three giant glamour shots mounted on the wall during his short stay there, all of the same woman, who I expected might be significant if still alive or around, and also possibly mortified to know she was on display in a care home like some sort of weird art installation. Jim would no doubt be along to take away these personal effects, so I asked the care home staff to box the photos for his friends to collect and I then just took the phone and the wallet.

Back in the office, the laminated tea wars sign hadn't worked, so they'd gone nuclear and moved the supplies from the kitchen cupboard to the table at our end of the office, next to the post tray. It remained to be seen how tenacious Housing would prove to be in their quest for free tea and coffee, having to now enter our territory to get it.

I started my usual round of calls and emails to the organisations who featured inside the wallet before charging up his phone and doing the surreal job of dialling the numbers, both from his address book and in the recent call log, to tell the random people who answered that the owner of the phone, whoever he was to them, was dead. Even though I had Jim, it was basic due diligence to make sure that no family were lurking out there.

I got varying reactions, from a very upset woman who needed a lot of comforting to a thoroughly indifferent man named Alan, who was more interested to know if I had found his camera in Matthew's stuff than discussing his demise. He'd borrowed it and hadn't given it back, he explained. He's probably filled it with sleaze and you wouldn't want it, I thought. I mentioned Jim as the main point of contact for the estate and he said 'Oh God, not that old jailbird.' Evidently, Jim had seen the inside of a cell too. I didn't probe any further.

A few days later when all the admin was completed and I was satisfied that there really was no next of kin, I arranged for Jim to come to the council offices and collect the phone and wallet, as well as the death certificates I had obtained after registering Matthew's departure. The registrar had come to enjoy my visits because of all the stories I brought about my people, to the extent where she had asked me to always book a double death slot when I made the appointment so she could hear all about the previous person's funeral and the next person's life. Though in this case she, like me, wasn't as enamoured as usual.

Jim kept me in reception for over an hour with some very manic and strange chat, more so than on the phone, his physical presence intensifying it. The customer services staff, again sensing something in much the same way as Catherine had in Matthew's room, kept hovering behind him and mouthing 'are you ok?' I would subtly nod that I was fine. Well, as fine as you can be chatting to someone who was being chillingly flippant about child abuse, but he was no immediate threat.

He mentioned that he was accessing Matthew's flat and taking things out to sell. I asked him not to do this as the funeral had the first call on the estate and until I had searched the flat it, like his bank account, was frozen. He defied this instruction by continuing to enter and clear things out over the coming days whilst I was awaiting access from the housing association. Notably, he removed Matthew's computer, claiming that it needed to be fixed. Yeah, I bet it did, I thought with a shudder. I was concerned again that I might be unfairly maligning poor old Matt here, but the backdrop being as it was, the computer suddenly being spirited away didn't feel like a coincidence. And anyway, I wasn't speaking ill of the dead, I was only semi-thinking it, and there is no saying precluding you from doing that. I resolved to stuff my personal feelings back down and plough on.

It's funny, a week before this case came in I had done some Section 46 funeral training with Steve back up in our London stomping ground. I had my first Pret lunch for many months and I was unduly excited, such a thing being entirely unattainable in my new one-horse town. The course leader had talked about protecting ourselves by being prepared for all eventualities during a house search. You don't know whose house you are entering, she said. These people may be in need of a council funeral because they were marginalised as socially unacceptable and their home may therefore contain some disturbing materials, such as the drawer full of hardcore child pornography she had opened when looking for the usual household paperwork. You can't unsee that kind of thing she said, with a slightly haunted look. It transpired that the guy was a paedophile who had been placed in the area upon release from prison and the locals had not taken kindly. Someone had set fire to his flat with him in it and killed him.

Wanting to get bang for my day trip to London buck, I had stayed at a friend's the night before and then booked a late train home so I could hit some galleries after the training. I liked nothing more than a yomp around all of the obscure hidden exhibitions in town and, like Carl, would often get lost for an entire day when I could.

Sometimes you hit magic, like an entire light and infinity mirror installation to yourself, or looking at a bucket on a plinth and having the artist jump out, ask you to put it on your head, then taking a photo to add to the gallery wall so you become the art. But sometimes you stand and stare at an electrified trumpet plugged into the mains, flipping a feather duster about on the floor and wonder what you're doing with your life. When everything was closed for the day I sat in a bar above the station and had two cocktails that were deceptively sweet and much stronger than I had bargained for. I then spent the two hour train ride home wistfully and slightly drunkenly staring out of the window, the pitch blackness meaning I was actually staring back in at myself and the reflection of the empty chairs around me.

I thought about everything that I had learned that day. The wording of Section 46 was interpretive. Very interpretive. To dispose of the remains. As a result, some of the councils in attendance didn't do a service, some kept it to a five-minute committal. The trainer cited one person who had attended the training in the past and told the room that he enforced the same service upon every client. Same reading and then Ave Maria, even if they loved Elvis. She had a stand-up row with him over that. One person proudly stated that they deliberately called it a pauper's funeral at their council, to put people off. Steve and I looked at each other several times over the course of the day, realising that we were in the minority. Taking photos of CD racks, books, vinyl, to find that perfect song and poem. When someone died in their car in our area, someone in the office grimly joked that they were driving in now, because word had spread about our service levels.

But back to Matthew and his suspicious aura. Despite this, it was still our duty to take care of him, the same as the trainer's convicted paedophile, the same as anyone else. And not in the loosest possible interpretation of Section 46, but properly. Whilst such a person would never warrant the affection I had for Jean, or the admiration I had for Carl, they would get the same service because it was my duty. Maybe dealing with both people I liked and people I didn't would help me find my emotional balance, I thought.

Thankfully, all Steve and I found in Matthew's flat were more smutty pictures he had taken of grown women, piles of bus magazines – he was big into them apparently and known to all the local drivers – and what we took to be Alan's camera, which I bagged and tagged to take to the funeral. With nothing of value in the flat and just enough in Matthew's bank account to cover his funeral costs, we gladly handed the keys of the property back over and told Jim he could fill his boots.

Even though I wasn't loving this case, it was at least proving mercifully simple. I had been saved the big job of establishing what was in the estate and who, if anyone, should stand to inherit it. There had been no need for anything more than a nominal house search, with none of the additional detective work required on top. Moreover my usual involvement in the development of the service was also voided by Jim and Richard deciding to stand down Martin and take on both the design and delivery themselves.

The plan, Jim told me, was for Richard to lead the service, as he was a retired priest. Obviously, I thought, before once again telling myself off for being particularly judgy throughout this one.

I expressed my doubts about a disgraced member of the clergy taking the service. It might reflect badly on the council that a funeral we were organising was being presided over by a twice-convicted paedophile. There might also be protests or outbursts from other attendees who knew of his background, or from locals who got wind, all of which could potentially derail the service and ruin the funeral. Even though I was not overly fond of Matthew, I had a duty to see to it that his send-off didn't descend into a slanging match or punch-up.

Jim, occupying his own parallel universe of propriety, disregarded everything I said and insisted it would go ahead as planned. I checked with my superiors about where we stood on dictating terms and, as I suspected, we could not refuse the involvement of a friend, particularly one whom the deceased had seen fit to leave half of his worldly goods to. The estate would be billed so the council tax payer would not be footing the cost, which protected us from the otherwise potential tabloid 'Council Funds Paedo Priest Funeral' headline.

Having made my peace with everything, as far as it was possible to do so, I went back to my normal day job until the funeral date rolled around. But even with my limited involvement, the case had created an inescapable aura of sleaziness that covered me like a light film of dust or layer of grease. Thankfully the funeral broke the spell due to it being so thoroughly strange and – it feels wrong to say this but here I go anyway – funny. It was akin to that thing where having watched a horror film late at night you need to flick around the channels and find something light-hearted like a comedy, or mundane like a weather report, as a sort of mood palate cleanse before you can go up the dark stairs to bed without being frightened anymore.

Thankfully it wasn't presided over by the dodgy ex-priest

in the end, in fact he didn't even turn up because, Jim told me, 'He decided that he couldn't come, he said he doesn't like crowds.' I should think he doesn't, I thought, especially those baying ones with pitchforks. And I didn't even mentally admonish myself for that one at this late stage, I just accepted that I was thoroughly jaded by the whole bloody thing. It was a strange revelation to suddenly have when he was all set to host it just hours before, so I think my cautionary words must have landed. I was glad to have potentially restored some dignity to Matthew on the off-chance he was just a naive innocent, or even if he wasn't for that matter.

Unfortunately this dignity was going to be short-lived as Jim was now taking the helm, with his peculiar character and speaking style; intense, frenetic, scatty, easily distracted, and often inappropriate. This was all further compounded by his being fairly unprepared, as Richard had only realised the evening before that he no longer liked crowds, and had bunged him a typed-up service to perform with no prior revision.

Jim was seemingly confident though, assuring me that he had excellent presentation skills. Having spoken to him for an hour I wasn't so sure, but as much as I wanted the funeral to go well, I had no right to refuse him and so, like Attenborough watching a lion about to savage a gazelle, I didn't meddle and let nature take its cruel course.

Jodie and the crematorium staff coached him a bit, took him into the chapel, showed him the set-up, talked him through the process; but really, there wouldn't have been enough dress rehearsals in the world.

The first omen was the funeral car of the person ahead of us breaking down, so we had a garish neon rescue vehicle parked in the space outside the chapel where the hearse pulls up. Poor old Matthew had to hang back for a bit whilst they finished tinkering with an engine before he could finally be driven up to the doors.

As the mourners – perhaps the wrong word because everyone was in civvies and very upbeat, it felt like a social club outing, but let's go with mourners – filed in, there were a pair of people sitting in the front row, wearing bright ski jackets and reading through the order of service for a good two minutes before realising they were at the wrong funeral and pushing their way back out to run across the graveyard from the crematorium to the neighbouring cemetery.

It's just as well we lost them as the funeral was very well attended, standing-room only in fact, with a large group of bus drivers taking up several rows. They had all arrived in an old routemaster which was set to take the other people to the wake afterwards. A nice touch which actually warmed my jaded heart a little bit. The other people were a very random assortment who all seemed quite offbeat and, as a consequence, remained thankfully oblivious to quite how strange everything that subsequently happened was. In that respect, the whole thing was a lot less problematic for me than it might otherwise have been. The person leading the funeral, everyone in attendance and the guy in the box, they were all quite singular, so the weirdness that followed was probably their baseline normal.

It took everyone ages to manage the simple task of filing

in, they were wandering off, drifting back out, all of them seemed as scatty as Jim. During this time he stood in the pulpit whilst an organist he had hired – who denied me and Steve our usual seat and had us standing behind him – played an awful dirge as Jim muttered, 'Come on, come on, what are you all doing?' as everyone dithered about and couldn't decide where to sit. When they were all eventually ushered into place by the crematorium staff he started doing, for want of a better descriptor, 'shout-outs' to people he could see in the room, along with some incidental facts about them – 'He used to live in Cheam' – before the staff, trying to keep the slot on track, announced sternly what Jim himself had been instructed to say once everyone was in but had forgotten to: 'PLEASE STAND.'

Jim spun around in surprise at this intervention, and as everyone slowly but duly obliged, he returned to his unfocused ways, playing with his papers and muttering to himself whilst Matthew was brought in and placed beside him. At this point he announced that he didn't know what to do now, and leafed through his notes before abandoning them and reading out verbatim from the order of service.

'The welcome… Oh yes, welcome… The tribute to Matthew… Ah yes, Matthew.'

The tribute was punctuated by a series of unintelligible tangents, my personal favourite being: 'I had a son, I held him in my arms and would have claimed him as my own but you know what they say, ménage a trois don't work,' followed by a reference to his 'strained undercarriage' and a loud sudden declaration that he was in his seventies but still did market research. He also pointed out the woman from the framed care home shots, and said, 'She's nervous about what pictures we have of her,' then laughed like a drain. At this point someone put their hand up and asked if we could all sit down as Jim had forgotten to do the 'be seated' bit after the earlier 'please stand'.

Every time he hit a different section of the service, he would announce it and then not know where it was in his notes. A woman in the front row would then run up to the pulpit and give him the correct page, kind of like in a theatre show where actors dry up and shout 'line!' I should add that he was doing all of this whilst covered in sellotape. He had brought name labels along for everyone – I don't know either – but they were poor quality and kept peeling back and falling off. So he got some sticky tape out of a giant bag for life he was hoofing around with him and covered his lapel and shoulder in it to keep his firmly on.

Then, after having to be prompted by front-row lady to say the words of committal – 'ashes to ashes', she had stage-whispered to him – he found it in his papers and read it off the page, as though it were the instructions for an Ikea bookcase. He then looked back up at us, paused, and with a beat of perfect comedy timing yelped, 'Now what?!'

Someone hissed 'Shut the curtain!'

He was meant to discreetly press a button whilst saying the committal, the idea being that during these touching words about the person returning to dust, the curtain would slowly envelop them, hiding them from our sight forevermore, and the service would be visually complete.

The words of committal hanging in the air, Jim then ducked down behind the pulpit, as though he'd seen a sniper, and banged about looking for the button. Front-row lady eventually ran up and pressed it for him and the curtain shut slowly and awkwardly to silence as he emerged looking dishevelled. The organist started up again with another tuneless dirge, but instead of everyone filing out in a reflective silence, Jim shouted logistical instructions about the wake at them from the pulpit. Does everyone have the postcode of the pub, for their satnav? There will be a cold buffet but if you want hot food you have to pay. All against a backdrop of sad organ music. He then finished with a line that no funeral has ever ended on before, I believe: 'Any questions?' So many questions Jim, so many.

Steve and I stood there as everyone left – finally able to let out a laugh having avoided eye contact for the whole thing in case we set one another off during the service – and pondered on whether what we had just seen counted as a massive failure or a massive triumph. Steve leaned towards the latter and gave an example of one council service he had arranged for an alcoholic who had been found dead in an underpass. The guy's fellow street drinkers had all attended and at the close of the service, had each poured a drink down onto his coffin. Steve had been worried that the one relative in attendance, a brother, might have found this upsetting, but he said that he actually found it very appropriate and strangely moving. Matthew was unconventional and his perfectly imperfect funeral reflected that. It certainly memorialised him; I'll never forget the experience and therefore the man.

As we drove away I thought about all of the atypical types of grief and mourner I had come across so far, so different from the pre-conceived familial norms. Care home staff, neighbours, garden club members, local bus drivers. There were a thousand ways to be mourned, the benchmark didn't have to be weeping spouses or devastated children. Nobody had shed tears that day, not even me for once, but they had packed the place out to the rafters and were all currently on a bus to a pub, united in their connection to this man and ready to raise a glass and a cold sausage roll to him, hot food at extra cost. Well, all except Alan, who was probably just there to claim his camera.

And as I sit here now and finish this chapter about an unusually mourned man, I have just learned that someone I knew solely online has taken their life this evening. A person I have never met but whose chatter was part of my daily backdrop for years and whose sudden brutal loss, their voice trailing off into the dark, has hit me like a gut punch. I feel a fraud for crying, they're not mine to mourn, but then none of my people are either and I have cried for some of them.

Days before I had seen them post that they were in a bad place and I dropped a supportive, if perfunctory comment, as you do when you are scrolling the non-stop noise, clicking *like*, *share*, commenting on a baby picture with the uniform 'aww'. Told him I was sorry to hear about his troubles and sent him my love. Not that my reaching out much more could have helped by the sounds of it, as though I could bring an internet acquaintance back from the brink.

The other arresting thing, as their voice falls silent, is the realisation that all of those anonymous voices I have become so used to, who actually represent a person and a life, will all gradually fall silent as time goes on. I knew this already, of course, look at my job, this book, but there's nothing like a practical lesson to bolster the theory. I barely grasped them in life, so their death is even more jarring in a way. From barely there to not there at all. Their last thought committed permanently to the internet, their photo still looking out at you, their continued presence in your friends list, along with their annual birthday reminder. It feels like they should start posting again at any moment.

As the early hours of the morning draw in and I field comments and messages from people wrestling with the same strange grief, as we all try to process this event in real time, talk about conversations we had with him, common interests we shared, recall how we found each other through him, I realise that we are having our own unconventional funeral tonight, though a lot less unusual than the one hosted by Jim.

I realise that head count at a funeral isn't the last judgement on our worth, that we can be mourned in many ways, by people we barely know, may never meet, with or without tears, just like my people. I realise that his experience became part of our collective experience, and that we take a part of that person with us going forwards, just as my people become part of my experience. And I realise that I am actually writing a book about life, not death; and living life through the oddly invigorating lens of death, perhaps all the better for it.

But death is the order of the day, and there are two more coming up now, namely Conor and Christian, after this short break.

Interlude

White. European. Female. Aged between 25 and 55. That was the extent of the detail. She didn't match any missing person's reports. Her DNA and dental records were a nil return. She didn't seem to exist anywhere.

After spending a year unclaimed in the morgue, she was released for burial. The referral came through under the name 'unidentified female'.

The only tangible thing I had to go on was itself completely intangible. An artist's impression of what she might have looked like. Her deep brown eyes were surely a scientific guess, as the front of her had been completely decomposed when she was found floating in the cove. Some hair had still been attached to her scalp, so the colour of that was accurate enough. Her face shape, too.

The expression was pure artistic licence of course, and it gave her a personality that the many people who became attracted to her story would, through the power of the picture and the feelings they projected onto it, come to actually believe was hers.

Serene, dignified, graceful, tragic.

There was a regal sternness there, like a benevolent medieval queen, and a slight flicker of a pre-Mona Lisa smile about to play across her face, but not quite yet. Mouth closed, keeping the secret of what had happened to her. All offset by an intense but kindly stare. So kind that I feel a strange friendship with her to this day. So intense that I can instantly summon her up at will if I close my eyes. Indeed throughout the case, her face, or rather the fictionalised version of it, frequently flashed into my mind, even entered my dreams.

The picture included the only other tangible clue. An antique necklace that she had been wearing when found, along with next to nothing else, just her bra. The picture redeemed the indignity of her ending. She was no longer the naked, rotting body in the sea who had surely perished in some terribly unpleasant way or another, whether at her own hand or that of someone else.

She was calm, content and restored.

But the picture wasn't real, the injustice of her end remained, and the final redemption was in my hands.

I resolved that this woman with no name, family or friends, would not be alone at the end; that her passing would not go unnoticed.

And it didn't.

Conor & Christian

Less than a month later, I arrived at the office to find two items in my pigeonhole. One was a letter from a bird-feeding complainant which contained pictures of pigeons. As I was the only one in, I made the obligatory pigeonhole – pigeons in my pigeonhole, geddit – dad joke to myself and then laughed; I was very tired. Whilst we're on the bird theme, just the day before we'd had an email entitled 'SEAGULL ATTACK', which contained no supplementary text, just a photo of a seagull outside someone's window and a video of the seagull tapping its beak on the window twice before flying off. I had resisted the urge to reply 'oh my God, are you ok?' and instead tactfully let them know that seagulls were wild animals so we couldn't serve a cease and desist notice on them; they would probably only eat it if we did.

The next item in my pigeonhole was something internal marked 'confidential'. Turned out my part-time request had been granted and I was working Monday to Wednesday, as of the following week. As delighted as I was to be thrown off the full-time treadmill into a life of long weekends, it was very sudden, and my first thought was, 'what if someone dies on my days off?' Well naturally the first couple of cases that came in were both referred on, you guessed it, a Wednesday afternoon, just as I was due to leave the office. It was like they were doing it on purpose.

Conor came in first, during the middle of what I later that day found out to be Dying Matters Week, so he was very on brand. It's one of those myriad awareness-raising hashtag affairs that pop up in your social media feeds on a near daily basis. There's one for every occasion, from Squirrel Appreciation Day to Sourdough September. This was one I could get behind, no offence to squirrels or sourdough. It was aimed at breaking the silence around death and getting people thinking about preparing, logistically and emotionally, for the end. The theme of the day was funeral costs. Very apt given that Conor's case was one of the surviving family having insufficient funds; it was to be my first case of this kind, and another on-the-job practical lesson. The costs motif was further reinforced by the £22 I had to pay for two death certificates. They had been £4 each the last time I had bought them and had more than doubled in cost overnight.

I hadn't been expecting the Grim Reaper to work according to my schedule, so had applied for my new hours resolving to stay flexible and, to this end, had set up a little grab bag in my locker containing everything I would need for an eleventh hour case. All of the forms and house search gear, sitting alongside my work shoes, cereal bars and Kit Kats, ready to be scooped up and taken home with me. I brought one back from work that night to get the case rolling in the morning, ahead of visiting the property come Monday.

I was due to return to my childhood hometown for a reunion that afternoon. A friend who had gone to live in Canada was back for a fortnight and we were revisiting the pubs we used to frequent back when we all worked at a local supermarket together as students. We ran the alcohol section and were given free booze if we averted any of the copious incidences of shoplifting that took place throughout the day. I worked evenings when it was most rife and at five foot nothing was the secret weapon, utilising the element of surprise. For example when five yoofs ran in, swiped a bottle of After Shock each and ran for the door, I let out a deep and blood curdling yell which stopped everyone in the store in their tracks. The kids froze and spun around. I stood there thinking, 'shit I've got to follow that up', but held my nerve and growled, 'you put that back.' Out of mostly confusion, they did. In the right place too, and that's an important detail because not even the nice shoppers do that. If they start to regret the cheese they picked up in aisle four, they dump it next to the bleach.

I got a free bottle of Kahlua for that display of bravery. But before I could head off and reminisce about this and much more, I got up super early, had a shower, and then set up at the kitchen table in curlers and a dressing gown to make my calls, hoping nobody would somehow sense my attire in my voice.

The surviving family of four sisters were a mix of pensioners and limited income earners, the latter group disentitling the entire clan from claiming DWP assistance. They had just lost another brother a couple of weeks earlier, and one of the sisters had terminal cancer herself. I spoke to the eldest who was understandably fragile and in some degree of shock. Her brother had not been unwell, his heart had just given out at the far from advanced age of 68. The first thing she did, through tears, was to apologise for wasting council money, something that stopped me in my tracks. Saddened and slightly angry that someone in the first throes of a loss was saying those words because of money or rather the lack thereof, it wasn't right. I told her that she should forget that and concentrate on her grief. Easier said than done.

In addition to feeling a burden, the process was being impeded by a huge sense of guilt that she was not able to do better for her brother. The stereotypical pauper's funeral imagery was strong with her and she had it in her head that the body would be taken away and burned in the night, with nobody allowed to attend. I'm not sure where the idea of the night in particular came from, I suppose it was just a fitting backdrop to the dismal image she had conjured up. Though I had read horror stories of councils not handing back ashes, refusing attendance at services, or not holding services at all, so it wasn't such a stretch. The relief when I mentioned the service of the family's devising was palpable. This was to be a proper funeral that allowed them to mourn, part of that mourning process being the involvement and planning. I felt slightly lighter when I rang off, and then immediately weary again as my next call was to his surviving long-term partner, so another difficult emotional one.

She had been with Conor for seven years but didn't live with him because it would have compromised both of their benefits entitlements. Once again it was depressing to see that money had dictated the manner of both life and death here. She stayed over now and then, sofa surfed the rest of the time. Come the end of the month, when Conor's now ex-landlord intended to sell up, she would have no solid base to return to and would be effectively homeless. It was a double blow, losing both her partner and the place they had spent many happy hours together. This was the first case where I had witnessed close-up the real aftermath of a loss, and just as I had felt myself approaching balance thanks to Matthew, I felt that wobble again. My referral forms were usually populated by information from a coroner or some other professional. Fielding this stuff from someone in distress was a huge leap and a steep learning curve.

At the end of the call I asked if there was anything else she needed. Get me a flat she had said, only half joking. As I didn't have much else to do on this case other than pop round to his property, then register the death and book the funeral, I accepted the challenge. As soon as I got off the call, I contacted our Housing and Homelessness team. They took her details, and those of the landlord and said they would arrange a meeting for the next week. They may have been alleged tea-bag thieves but they got the job done.

The following Monday I visited Conor's flat with our Community Warden Dan, who was the only person in the office when I arrived and so by default had to answer the bat signal with me. I was slightly nervous on the drive across. House searches were always done in empty anonymous properties, not with someone connected to the deceased sitting on the sofa watching. I didn't want to cause upset as I rifled through drawers and took photos. Dan had been a bailiff in his last job and was well used to approaching properties with trepidation, albeit of a different kind, and so had hardened himself over the years. He was a good person to have along; a steadying, official and disconnected presence to anchor myself against.

We pulled up to the house and Conor's partner let us into what turned out to be a very small and sparsely furnished upstairs flat. I was relieved as I subtly scanned the main room into which we were invited to sit and saw nothing of any value. No cash on the sideboard, hardly any possessions, sparsely furnished. I wouldn't have to seize and decant any goods into evidence bags in front of a bereaved person, always a bonus. Dan remarked afterwards that he had done the same scan upon entering but with his bailiff's eye which, had it been that kind of a job, would have been conversely disappointing.

Not seizing items didn't make it all that much easier of course, I still had someone sitting next to me on the sofa crying. I couldn't just take his bank statements and leave to start work on the case as I usually would. This was a perfect example of the job not staying within the lines of the on-paper description. The written guidance on how to complete the search didn't cover this. She was on her own in the place he had died, about to be made homeless, and needed to talk to someone. I listened, offered what I could in terms of understanding and (very) basic human insight, making a mental note at one point that I would quite like some bereavement training. We stayed for as long as we reasonably could, Dan having another job to get to, and me having a fair amount of death admin to get started. If you've ever found it difficult to find the right moment to leave a social engagement, imagine that but times a million.

A couple of Wednesdays later, on the eve of Conor's funeral, as I was about to leave the office for the week, along came Christian. To be fair to him, he had actually died three weeks earlier so he wasn't trolling me, the police were. Rather unusually, I received an email from the coroner, instead of a call, and it came with a large portion of too much information. Under the request there was the police report with a full description of the scene that they had broken down the door and stumbled into. It did at least tip me off that I would need to take all of my protective gear. I noticed that the date of the police report matched Christian's date of birth, and sighed. They had found him on his birthday.

This one would clearly involve more than a few phone calls at home in my jimmy-jamas; a full house search was called for. The poor guy had been dead for nearly a month. I had an #engagement through #socialmedia course the following Monday, so that I could produce excellent #content for service promotion. I couldn't leave him almost another week until Tuesday. I had already been planning on going to Conor's funeral the next day anyway, so I decided to go for broke and visit Christian's property afterwards. I was really starting to blur the lines between my life and my job, but it was hard not to, when the job was not a job, it was life, well death, well both. It was another area where I would need to find balance, I thought to myself as I left the office with my trusty funeral grab bag once again. I then drove home mentally planning the following day – dentist, funeral, house search – then my route and my costume changes.

The next morning I was in the dentist's waiting room nice and early, dressed like a professional mourner, checking in for a long-standing appointment I had booked before everybody died. While we waited for the anaesthetic to take effect, he asked me about my Morticia attire. I explained I was going to a funeral, briefly forgetting that most people go exclusively to the funerals of those whom they know and love, so after a beat, and before I got any undeserved sympathy, I quickly explained the circumstances and then asked if I would still be numb in an hour's time because I didn't want to slur my condolences.

As I arrived at the crematorium the dentist's promise came good and I felt my mouth returning to near normal. I was slightly early so I said a quick hello to the celebrant. Martin wasn't available so I had gone with Jodie's back-up lady. Conor's partner had said how lovely she had been to her, taking a lot of time to develop the service and incorporate meaningful stories and details, and how much this interest and empathy had helped; I let her know. I then snuck off for a walk around the graves, complimenting one dead person out loud on the unique raised flowerbed design of their final resting place, and looking for Angela, so I could see her next to her husband and say hello. I wondered as I wandered, were my attachments to my people just because I was a handful of cases in? Would I ever get so far into the job that I would forget my previous people, move on from them altogether? What was Dunbar's number when it came to relationships with the dead?

I only had ten minutes until the funeral, and my turn around the graves nearest to the chapel had brought no success, so I briskly returned to the crematorium building, via the children's cemetery, which was simultaneously the saddest and sweetest of places, full of toys, balloons and an impressive Lego castle built upon one grave. As I passed through I briefly thought about my dad's brother, who had died in infancy of dehydration. His death had tipped my dad off that I was dying of the same thing myself as a baby and is what ultimately saved my life, as my parents staged a sit-in at the hospital until emergency surgery was performed.

Every day on the way to work in my previous life I had passed the graveyard where my uncle – strange to call a tiny baby that – was buried, and it always served as a sobering reminder that I should already be long gone, was lucky not to be, but before I got too cocky, that it was ultimately just a temporary reprieve, and the grave would be waiting. I don't mean this in a sinister way. Rather than a dark foe that could strike at any time, I just see it as a bland event, as likely and routinely to arrive as a bus. Yeah, maybe I was made for this job.

As I emerged from the rose-covered pergola walkway that led to the chapels, I was taken aback by a large crowd of people outside the one we were using. I wondered if there was a mix-up as there was a bigger chapel just around the corner. I then recognised Conor's partner at the front of the crowd. Upon seeing her it clicked. I had only dealt with his partner and sisters, so my brain was expecting to see just them. I'd had no dealings with the celebrant, no clues to impart, or people I had discovered to link in. Everyone in attendance had been invited by his loved ones. The crowd, I learned during the eulogy, was an entire local pub's worth of friends. They packed the pews out, so I sat in my now usual organ overflow seat. As I had gone straight from home on my day off, it was just me, no Steve, and as it started, I felt slightly exposed without him.

My previous case being Matthew, whom it had been quite hard to love, and my lack of direct involvement in the planning of this one, had given me a phantom notion of a burgeoning professional distance that evaporated the second The Carpenters' 'Close to You' started up.

The partner and the sisters collapsed into tears and I, for the first time, heard all about Conor, and found out through the eulogy the things I would have usually discovered for myself on the journey that would have connected me to the case, and in turn to him.

This was not a Section 46, this was a family funeral and I was about to witness huge amounts of grief, and catch some of it too, because you can't not. I slid my sunglasses down from the top of my head as I welled up, and resigned myself to probably not getting any better at this stuff, and a good thing too.

As I left the service, I collected myself, thanked the celebrant, and stopped to give my professional condolences to the family, but of course cried as soon as the sisters and partner hugged me. It was so proper, they said, slightly stunned. The coffin, it was actually, nice. I knew exactly what they meant. It took me back to my first experience with Jean. The coffin wasn't cardboard, the chapel was the same one everyone else used, the celebrant was a professional. Conor had been given a proper funeral, and as much as they were devastated, there was a lightness in their voices that I hadn't heard in the run-up. In the partner's case, this was also due to the fact that the Housing team had helped her to stay on in Conor's flat by buying it from the landlord and making it part of their social housing stock. They had more than earned that free tea. I left the funeral as happy as you can be when you're, you know, leaving a funeral, heartened by the thought that money didn't end up robbing him or his family of their right to grieve with dignity, and grateful that my job and the council made this possible for anyone who died in this way.

I took a moment to shake off the morning and then drove to the next town to start the process all over again, like some sort of bleak Mary Poppins, to see what Christian's story was. Once parked up I lay down in the back seat wriggling out of my long black funeral skirt and into my jeans. I left my black top on, black goes with anything luckily for me. Costume change complete, I got my grab bag from the boot and went looking for the property, and for Steve who was meeting me there after his morning visits. I was back to familiar ground with this one. No family, no raw emotions, just me and Steve wandering around in a silent place full of clues. The only people Christian seemed to know were a firm of independent financial advisers who occupied the office space in front of his flat. I had visions of a surreal funeral with just us, some indifferent businessmen, and a eulogy about how they got him a great deal on a re-mortgage.

When we went into the offices there was a bit more to it, as there seemingly always is in life. The director had known Christian for thirty years and considered him a friend. Not a close friend, but it wasn't possible to be close friends with Christian, he was very aloof and didn't stop and chat. Despite a three decade-long relationship, he was unclear if Christian even had any family or other friends. He had only ever seen him in the company of one woman, he didn't know her name and she hadn't been around for a couple of years now. Christian had mental health problems he told us, specifically schizophrenia, and he signed off all of his letters with 'God save the King'.

'I'll be interested to see what you find in there,' he said. Christian never invited anyone inside his flat. I was now very curious myself.

As I was taking notes, the director asked us about the job and about the other cases we had done. He seemed to want to keep us for longer and go beyond the basic fact-finding chat about Christian. He eventually worked up to the thing he wanted to talk about: his grief. He was shaken by the simple fact of feeling it. As someone who had just recently grieved for an online acquaintance, I knew what he meant, and suggested that losing someone fairly peripheral but constant could hit harder than we expect. It's a strange category of loss. You're ready to mourn family or spouses, you know that day is coming, it will hurt but it won't surprise. To get a stab of grief however, when you least expect it, is unsettling. The incidental deaths of acquaintances or colleagues, even celebrities, people gradually dropping off, it can lead to an existential wobble as those who make up the general furniture of your life disappear. Your life is in turn slowly diminished, until ultimately you leave it too. Even the extremely peripheral deaths of my people seemed to keep me on my existential toes.

The director walked us round to the flat, handed over the key and started back towards his office. When he was out of sight we cracked the door, expecting the infamous death smell to hit us full in the face, but we were – I don't want to say pleasantly surprised, because the death smell that was still lingering there, and would do so until the carpets were removed, could not in any way be termed pleasant – relieved, I suppose, to see that the windows had been cracked by the police, and the fresh air had helped matters enormously. We could forego the face masks. We went into the room where he had died and the scene was not as bad as expected, just the usual brown black patch, so we could also forego the haz suits I had lugged along to the funeral in my handbag and just wear the gloves and shoe covers.

It was a small flat, almost a bedsit. We did a walk around, scooped the post up from the doormat – a couple of birthday cards that he never got to open – cleared out the fridge, just in time as there were some crab sticks on the turn, and then started the search.

We took one side of the main room each; Steve going through a bookcase and cupboard, me going through a desk and wardrobe, chatting through what we found. A lot of these house searches involve a fair degree of admiring people's books, decorations, music and so on. In this case we got to hold up and remark upon a lot of notebooks with densely-written pages of what looked like quantum mathematics. Christian seemingly had a brilliant mind. This was further borne out by some letters from various science journals thanking him for submitting articles or theories, and a membership pack for the Royal Astronomical Society. Every person came with a unique skill, angle or story. He was rich too, with several bank and building society statements showing six figure balances. His wealth didn't show in his home though, it was all threadbare furniture and mess. He had hardly any food in and very few possessions. It didn't feel in any way tragic, just a possible side-effect of his apparent genius, too busy studying and theorising to cook, amass possessions and keep house I thought, and hoped.

There were dozens of packets of photographs in the desk drawers. Typically paydirt for clues, but not on this occasion. I flicked through the first pack to no avail, then picked up another, and flicked and flicked, then picked up another and so on. Steve noticed my silence, confused squinting and wrinkled nose. 'What they of?' he asked warily, possibly remembering the training example.

'Oh, nothing bad, just a bit odd, I think they're all of his phone screen.' I handed a packet over and Steve flicked through, joining me in pulling the same face, and concluded that I was right, it was just photo after photo of different images of his phone screen. We eventually concluded that he had taken an unorthodox approach to backing up his phone's camera roll; by taking grainy physical photos of everything on there. He was clearly scientifically brilliant but not of the Cloud generation.

There were a couple of framed photos on display around the flat, both of the same woman, probably the woman the director had mentioned, I suggested. I picked one up and turned it over. Christian had written 'Anya, my first love' on the back. I shared this very on-the-nose clue with Steve and put the photo in a pile we were developing on the bed from our respective search areas to take back to the office.

Once I had finished searching the desk and wardrobe I spotted a metal box wedged between them. I dragged it out and prised it open. It was full of dividers and folders, always promising, people only use dividers for official stuff. The dividers theory came good as I pulled out a will and a paid-up funeral plan. I think I may have even said 'wahey' as I waved it at Steve, such was my relief at knowing what he wanted after a quite patchy search, paperwork-wise.

The will dealt with his wealth, bye bye Treasury Solicitor, and the plan drilled down so far that it even stated his preferred church and detailed wishes for the service. Sissel Kyrkjebø's 'Funeral Song' to start. Her rendition of 'Going Home' to close. Liam Clancy's 'The Parting Glass' in the middle. It also expressed a wish that he be buried with Anya. 'Well, that explains why she hadn't been seen for a couple of years then,' said Steve.

'Yeah, wow, he must have been very aloof if he didn't mention the existence and subsequent death of the first and possibly only person he ever loved.'

'Or so heartbroken he couldn't talk about it?' We paused and decided to just take comfort in the fact he had loved, even if he had lost.

With enough paperwork to be going on with, Steve headed off and I took the evidence bag back to the office. First things first, I phoned the funeral company to activate the plan. What I had thought would be a simple transaction immediately faltered as I was told that Christian was covered for cremation only. I pointed out the line under 'extra information' which said 'burial requested' and his extra notes about said burial being with Anya.

'Oh no,' the woman said. 'That would all count as additional and fall outside of the plan.'

I saw what had likely happened. He had been sold a cremation package and had believed that his wishes that were added to the extra information notes were included in that. If I wanted to upgrade him to a burial they would contribute £600 towards the costs, which was nothing in the grand scheme of funereal things. Slightly fuming on his behalf at this possible mis-selling, I needed a moment and said I would call them back. In the meantime, I made some other calls in the hope something came up. A family member who could take it on and carry out his wishes, or some other magic solution. It was now five o'clock and other colleagues who were actually at work that day were starting to pack up and go home around me. My dead people get service, mate.

Christian's address book was full of entries that had been Tipp-ex'd out with the word 'dead' written over the top. It reminded me of a birthday card I was sent by a family friend as a kid, where her husband's name was scratched out in red pen on account of the fact he had died shortly after signing it, which kind of made it look like she had murdered him and was crossing him off her kill list. The remaining numbers were just plumbers, MOT garages and the like. Almost out of options, I dug out his passport and flicked to the back. There were two people given as emergency numbers. Bingo! Emergency numbers have to be family, right? Well, in this case, wrong. The first was a woman who sold him vitamin supplements. She seemed very confused about him naming her as a crisis contact, as was I, but said she would certainly go to the funeral, so that was something.

The second number was a solicitor's office. Another dead end, I thought. Though as I chatted to the named person, it turned out she had helped him when buying Anya's grave. The grave he wanted to go in. She had the paperwork to prove ownership too, if I wanted it. Oh. Yes. Please. She had also heard of me through one of my cases that had made the news.

'Can I just check, are you the woman from the radio? Wow, I'm in one of your cases!' And now she's saying that in my book too, how meta.

That very useful call took care of one of the biggest costs, the plot, but £600 was still going to bring us in under budget.

I sat there and considered my quandary. The cremation plan covered collection, care, coffin, service, celebrant, cremation and urn. It would be the easiest thing in the world to activate it and do everything for free, but this would go against Christian's true wishes, so was an obvious no-no. I could certainly bury him, to ensure his manner of disposal was honoured, but it would be in a different cemetery and not in a dedicated plot with Anya. I also couldn't take up the burial contribution because my contracted funeral home wasn't in the plan company's network, so they would get away with mis-selling a plan and pocketing all the cash. I looked around and realised it was now just me and Kath the cleaner left in the room. I needed to get this concluded before Facilities locked up for the day.

Head spinning and starting to ache, I phoned the independent financial advisers and explained the two undesirable options and the two ideas I had to solve this problem. Firstly, enact the funeral plan and then take his ashes from the council and inter them privately with Anya, not ideal but as close to his wishes as a council funeral could get under the circumstances. Or secondly, something I had remembered from my Institute of Cemetery and Crematorium Management training. Take the funeral back off me and book a private affair, which one of his brimming-with-cash bank accounts could be invoiced for in advance of the funeral. They could additionally claim his rightfully owed £600 and he would be back with Anya within a matter of weeks. To my immense relief they chose the latter. I emailed over the interim death certificate along with the proof of grave ownership and was home just an hour and a half late for tea, my confidence in the job once again increased by having had to improvise a solution to the funeral riddle, and my contentment restored as another customer got the right ending and joined the Conga line of souls gathering behind me who I'd been able to help out.

Before bed I emailed the coroner to let him know about the conclusion and also note some things we had observed during the house search which might help him with the inquest – some medicines and a letter complaining about an ongoing illness – fully expecting him to pick it up in the morning. He replied straight away.

'What are you doing online at this time of night?' I asked.

'I could ask you the same thing,' came the response. Fair. Our jobs, unlike our clients, never slept, we agreed. They were about death, which ties in with life and therefore covers just about everything, barring the afterlife, so it was impossible to just put on an out-of-office and forget.

Deciding that this week was not destined to be part-time, I took Christian's will, papers and photos back to the independent financial advisers the next day to sign them back over. I then went to collect Conor. His family didn't have a car to get back to the crematorium with and claim his ashes, and two taxi rides that far out would have been prohibitively expensive for them. I wasn't sure what to expect, so I walked into reception with a shopping bag full of bubble wrap. He was actually presented to me in one of those glossy gift bags you get in nice shops, the ones with the rope-effect handles that make you feel better about buying something overpriced. I was surprised at the hefty weight for such a small box, but then I supposed it was a whole person after all, and very densely packed too.

Whilst signing him out, I asked if they could help me locate a grave. I had a bit of time before my appointment to drop the ashes at the funeral home, from where his family would be in walking distance to pick him up at their convenience, and I wanted to actually find Angela this time. The guy remembered her case, having been one of many copied in on the Lord's final ultimatum email.

'That was quite a to-do,' he said, in the serene and understated tones of someone who talks to the bereaved all day and can't quite shake the habit even when joking. I've found that with bereavement helplines for banks too. I'll call up, announce that I'm from the council and need to freeze an account under Section 46, and the staff still keep up the sympathetic tones, peppering the conversation with 'aw' and 'bless' and even offering me their condolences. It becomes a well-intended verbal tic after a while, I suppose. He went out the back and returned with a map and a pen, then highlighted her grave for me and drew a walking route.

The Jewish section was small, but I still managed to wander past her a couple of times. She only had a tiny stake identifying her location. I wasn't expecting her to have a stone yet, what with the whole sinking issue I mentioned earlier, but I had however been hoping to find her by looking for her husband's stone. He didn't have one either though, or even a stake anymore. His grave was just an outline of once-disturbed grass. I guess a stone would have been a stretch when those burying him were doing so out of inherited duty and duress. At least they had found each other again. I told them I was happy to see them together, then added a qualifying, 'Obviously not happy you're both dead and in a grave, just, yeah, you guys know what I mean.' I then shook my head at my creeping habit of talking to nothing and walked back to the car, stopping to watch a departing mourner reverse into a gravestone twice as I went, and then popped Conor in my boot as respectfully as one can do such a thing.

I drove past his flat on the way to the funeral home and wondered what he would have made of it all if a mere month ago when he was still alive, someone had told him that he would cease to exist in a matter of weeks, and that a stranger would be driving past his front room shortly thereafter with his ashes in her car boot along with some shopping bags, bubble wrap and beach shoes. This could be true of any one of us though, I thought with an existential shudder. Except for the ending up in my car boot bit, that would be scarily specific, and also dodgy on my part. But seriously, you too could be walking around with a month left on your clock, hopefully not, but we all have an invisible deadline, pun fully intended, that we are counting down to.

Which brings us back to the week Conor died, bang in the middle of: Dying Matters. If you were to get hit by the proverbial bus tomorrow, would anyone know what you wanted? Didn't want? Who you bank with? Where your paperwork is filed? How to get into your phone? And a million more questions besides. All of which you will no longer be there to answer. Unless you make like Christian and I, and create a neat file of information, wishes and the paperwork to go with them.

Having to make educated guesses about cremating or burying has been a source of worry for me throughout this job, so make your wishes known, both in the formal framework of a will and in clear instructions, both verbally and perhaps even with a supplementary written note. My will says cremate me, but my extra note in the folder where I have all my documents says direct cremation, no fuss, no gold handles that I will be too dead to enjoy. Or if that exciting new freezing and shattering technique makes it over from the States, then obviously that instead, please. Don't let your surviving relatives, partner or friends get up-sold on a fancy coffin that you would be aghast at them wasting their cash on. There can be a lot of guilt swirling around in the wake of a loss that people try and make good on with lavish flowers and five-stretch limos. Give your people something solid and definite that they can go in there with, that allows them to remain impervious to the offer of added extras, because they are bolstered by your wishes.

For those left behind, before you walk into the nearest funeral directors, check the prices on their website. There was a new rule enacted in 2021 that compels them to display this information. Better yet, save yourself time by going to the 'Your Funeral Choice' website first. Yes, even funerals have comparison sites, but no funny meerkat mascots because that would just be crass. When searching my own area I found price differentials of over £1,000, so it's worth shopping around. It's not a purchase we make that often, hopefully anyway, so whereas we know what we're prepared to pay for a pint of milk, we've no idea what to expect for a funeral package. This is further compounded by the fact that, at such a time, people probably aren't feeling up to shopping around, popping into loads of branches and re-hashing the same painful conversation. It's not exactly the fun kind of shopping, and it's something that people really just want done and over with so they go into the first available branch and accept the price without question.

Of course you can avoid funeral director fees altogether and go down the DIY route. It's a little known fact that you don't legally have to use a funeral director. You can order coffins or shrouds online and you can care for the body at home and bring it to the cemetery or crematorium yourself. Upon learning this, I started seriously considering requesting a basic shroud and being driven shotgun to the crematorium, Weekend at Bernie's style. You can also bury the body on private land, provided you follow certain rules, which can be found on the 'Natural Burials' website. Another workaround is to opt for direct cremation, where the body is taken away, cremated and the ashes returned by post. You can then perform your own personal – and free – service when you scatter them.

If you are struggling with money to the extent that any personal cost would be too onerous, the DWP offers some limited help, as I mentioned earlier, and there are also a number of charities who can offer supplementary assistance. Quaker Social Action's 'Down to Earth' charity can help link you in with them and also help you to claim anything you are owed by the government or any charitable assistance available. And of course, the council is always here.

You might also want to consider the content, after all it's your funeral. Think about songs and readings that mean something to you. In a typical service there will be a song on the way in, a song in the middle, and a song on the way out. You might want to jot down a selection to choose from. You might even want to write your own eulogy. My mum's best friend found out she had four brain tumours and a month to live. She created a three tab spreadsheet of funeral tasks – who to invite, who to give things to, hymns, poems, prayers – and dictated her eulogy to her daughter after she lost her sight. It made things a lot easier in the aftermath of her death. It helped her to die well too, master of her own demise. She also asked for her mobile phone to be put in the coffin and for us to ring it during the service, so it's a bonus chance to be genuinely hilarious one final time.

And there ends the death lecture inspired by the thoughts I had during Dying Matters week, the week when Conor ceased to exist in life, but turned up in my workload and then my car boot, and the month where Christian turned up and showed us all how it was done. With my first family funeral under my belt, and the – soon to be the next PPI scandal, surely – over-fifties life cover people thwarted, I was feeling increasingly confident in my professional chops. My next case however would test my fledgling mettle by making things truly personal. Enter Mark.

Mark

During the lulls between cases, work life would return to normal. Normal within the parameters of the job that is. I would lurch from complaints from people having their 'lives blighted by the rogue peacock' who would go on to claim that the owner had 'washed their hands of it, saying it has gone feral' to ringing the bell at a speed-dating briefing event for new councillors. Despite the format being explained, nobody, to a person, paid any attention to me and so I ended up just being a woman standing in a room ringing a bell every three minutes to no avail, for an hour. It should have been longer but a few people had to leave early to get to Morris-dancing practice, so I was saved and reminded of how far from my stressful city job I had come.

I also had time to do a bit of training and spent three full days in a bland suburban hotel meeting room studying the Licensing Act 2003, with no biscuits. Inhumane. Then a day up in London studying the DWP funeral payment process (and yomping around more galleries afterwards, one was in a crypt, very on-brand) because my first lack of funds referral had given me pause. Whilst I was sure I had been correct in my assessment of Conor's next of kin eligibility, or lack thereof, I was aware that it had been based in large part on asking Google after the main DWP site had left me confused.

If it had left me confused in my neutral state of mind, I couldn't imagine how someone in financial distress and in the wake of a loss would possibly navigate it. If I was going to lead on this area, I needed schooling in order to guide others and hopefully empower them to make their own arrangements so they wouldn't have to feel the way Conor's sisters and partner had felt in the first days of calling upon me, and indeed had probably felt right up until the funeral had proved not to be as meagre as they had feared.

My preconception of the process being akin to solving a bridge troll's riddles was confirmed as I was given a heart-sinking flow chart wherein nearly every arrow went on a strangled route before ultimately leading back to 'claim denied'. At least I could field people's situations, I thought, hand back control to those very few who qualified, and stop those who didn't from wasting their time on an abortive claim that elongated the duration between the death and their ability to focus on grief instead of admin.

As I said at the top, everyone in the family, including step and adoptive, have to be on a qualifying benefit to receive the payment, which is very rare, though not entirely unheard of. The next family who came to me very much qualified had already been around the houses to get to me and were too tired to start filling out long forms – and believe me, it is a long form – which would take a further month to process, during which time they would have to front the deposit all funeral directors require, and which they couldn't afford. All options explained, from the DWP route, to cheap funerals, to charitable options, and the man said, 'No, we want to do it through you please, free, through you, for nothing please.' I found the phrasing slightly odd but was quite happy to take him on. Happier still that the curse of the Wednesdays had been broken and I had three whole days to get this show on the road.

The person he was calling about was his brother-in-law, Mark, who had died of cancer in a care home, palliative, not residential. He had been in a supported living flat up until that point. My fledgling confidence in dealing with cases which involved relatives was briefly rattled when he explained that Mark had a learning disability and added that Mark's only surviving blood relative was his wife, Mark's older sister. I myself was an older sister to a learning disabled brother and felt instantly too close to the case for comfort.

I had often had cause to think about his, and my own death. He came along when I was two, and had been brain damaged by a traumatic birth. In the months and years that followed, everything was geared towards ensuring his safety and security in the world after myself and my parents died. I never got the gateway death of a hamster as a starter for ten, I went straight to contemplating those of everyone around me and then myself. Which probably explains a lot about me, both now and then. When I was two, I stood up on a plane seat during take off and declared 'We're all going to die!' Still very much my vibe. At five, my mum found a list in my dungarees pocket when she was doing laundry, and asked me what it was. 'Things I need to do before I die,' came the answer. I knew I was on the clock from the off and have been in a massive hurry ever since. One of the ambitions on my kiddy bucket list was to go on more buses, something I am proud to say that I have achieved. Follow your dreams, guys. Another one was to live in Cockleshell Bay. Entirely unachievable as it was a stop-motion animated children's show in the early 1980s, but living by the sea is not too far off.

After seeing the way the world treats the disabled I have always wished, in a strange way, that my brother would die before me, so that I can die myself knowing he won't be alone and at the mercy of cruel or opportunistic people; a grim wish but one driven by love. I wondered if the sister in this case had the same complex feelings about her disabled brother predeceasing her as I was anticipating with mine. I wondered if we would get to talk about it.

Details taken and work head back on, the first order of business was to retrieve Mark's body, which had been sent many miles away to a funeral director in his hometown. I looked back in my files to see if the care home he was sent there by had received our letter stating they would bear the costs if they carted off Section 46 clients to any old place. They had, so I got on the phone preparing to tell them this one was on them, and then to arrange my now awkward-under-the-circumstances visit. They informed me that Mark, realising he was dying, had called for his priest and made his last wishes known. He wanted a funeral through this particular company, who had dealt with those of both his parents, and a service at his local church, led by his parish priest. The trouble was, Mark's family didn't have the money for any of this. Maybe he didn't even realise it was something that cost money. My brother has no concept of it. If you ask him how much a banana is, he'll say ten pounds. He will give the same answer for a BMW convertible. I couldn't therefore bill the home, who were just enacting wishes in good faith, and so asked our funeral director to collect him and put it on our tab.

Mark located and rescued, I set off to the care home to search his room. Steve was off and everyone else was tied up, so I made the call to head off by myself. Care home rooms usually reap no valuables and I could get the nurse to watch me and co-sign for anything I found.

When I arrived, I was getting my rubber gloves on in preparation to be shown to the room when I was called in by the manager. No point taking them off now, I thought, and headed in looking like a strangler and thinking I was going to get some aggravation for the earlier call about the body removal fee. But no, she was very friendly, offered me tea even, chatted to me for a bit about Mark, his wishes as he had articulated them in his final hours, the type of service, the hymns and where he wanted his ashes scattered. It was odd as this was all stuff I had noted down over the phone earlier, and managers really don't have time for this. Her phone, like the manager at the last home I went to, was ringing off the hook the whole time too, but she was ignoring it. My hands were getting sweaty at this point and I needed to get on so I went quiet in order to Louis Theroux-her into saying whatever it was she was clearly trying to get to. After an awkward silence she finally said '…They tried to get him to sign his body over to medical science, the family.' I stayed quiet, not sure what to say, and motioned for her to go on.

'Before he died, they visited with forms for him to sign. He signed them because they told him to. They needed to be counter-signed by his GP. When I took them away and read them, I went straight back to his room, explained to him what he just had signed and checked that he was ok with it. He wasn't. He was horrified, really upset, and tore it up. When I told them the next day, they were angry. They said the matter had been settled, but it hadn't, not with him. I thought you should know.'

My misty-eyed thoughts of having a cosy conversation about disabled siblings evaporated right there and then.

From a brief foray onto a siblings forum many years before, I knew that some saw their disabled brother or sister as a burden, some even as a non-person, whose perceived pointless yet imposing existence was a great irritant. Might that be the case here? There were FAQs on the site about how to avoid being seen in public with them and how to get time away from them with just the parents. I deactivated my account with that disturbing pity party more or less immediately, but not before advising them that their FAQs should be amended to include the option of developing some character.

Mark

As challenging as it can be, and it really can be – I mean the number of my personal possessions my brother has put down the toilet doesn't bear thinking about – it's never dull. His mood changes depending on whether he is hot, tired, hungry, like all of us, I suppose, but he has no filter, so he will go from telling me I'm beautiful to telling me to fuck off to asking me for a milkshake and demanding I play him 'It's Raining Men', his favourite song, that I have to keep on repeat when he is round for a curry and a beer. He loves colourful pants and socks and when he asked if he could show me his new pants one time, I, expected him to carry them into the room, was treated to a middle-aged man running in, hands on hips, thrusting his bright yellow Y-fronts at me.

He insists on having his birthday cake candles relit umpteen times and makes us all watch as he blows them out again and again. Except he can't blow, he has seen people blow and apes the motion, thrusting his head forward and pursing his lips, but explaining that he needs to summon air and push it out of his mouth has never made sense to him, so we all have to surreptitiously do it for him and then clap him for our own work.

When we went to a festival where there was a giant inflatable whale, he ended up leaning his head against it for ages saying 'aw I love him' and he frequently decides he loves soft toys that he sees in shops, making us buy them for him and naming them all Smithy. I'm going to go out on a limb and say it's more interesting than your average sibling relationship.

He is also the binary opposite of me in that he has

no concept of death, that I am aware of. Only really understanding language in a very literal sense, for example, indignantly claiming that he is 'being have' when he is told to behave, and using the same words and phrases on rotation, a bit like 'Station' in Bill and Ted's Bogus Journey, so it's safe to assume that deeper concepts and meanings are beyond him. If you can't explain to him how to blow out a candle or blow his nose – poor boy just has to sit there throughout any cold or 'flu streaming – you aren't going to be able to tackle metaphysics.

When people die – and many did in his youth at his special needs school, their life-limiting conditions coming as part and parcel of their disability, going home one day and never coming back – he would file them away in the last place he saw them and chat to them as he lay in bed at night. You know he's gone to sleep when his babbling conversation with old classmates and dead grandparents drifts off and finally ceases.

When my aunt was dying she wanted to become one of the ghost people he chatted to, so she bought a bird bath for the garden at his home. The garden is one of the other places where he chats away to people as he pushes a wheelbarrow around, usually empty, he isn't in it for the transporting, he likes the motion. Her note, that he couldn't read, or comprehend when I read it to him, said: 'I bought this for you so I can always be there with you, and you can talk to me in the garden with grandma and granddad.' He stared off and then asked if he could put his socks on and go out in the car. I cried; the major differences between us illustrated there.

Mark

I was shown to Mark's room where the bed had been stripped and his bags packed and piled on top. The only thing of significance was his wallet, all else was clothes, puzzle books and a huge stash of Kit Kats, and I mean huge, every variety thereof too, from classic, to flavoured, to chunky. His wallet didn't contain much, but there were a couple of things to close down so I showed the nurse the contents, made her sign my itinerary, and bagged it. There was a coffee shop loyalty stamp card in there which was completed. He never got his free beverage. This is why I always claim my rewards straight away, I thought. I want to leave life up on the deal.

When I got back to the office, I did my usual closing and freezing of memberships and accounts respectively, knocking up premises licence variations whilst on hold so I didn't fall behind in that area of my work and shouting out the odd quiz answer across the room: 'Scrooge McDuck... Sorry, not you, I'm calling from the council.' When I phoned the bank, the bereavement line woman went from the traditional 'aw bless' every other word, even in response to my confirming the sort code, and actually broke character when confronted with his account details.

'Sorry,' she said, 'I need to put you on hold again, there are a lot of direct debits here, an unusual amount, like, I've never seen this many, this account will take a long time to freeze.' A subsequent call to his key worker also cast doubts on the appropriation of his money. As with the care home manager, she lowered her voice and confided in me that he had been asked to write cheques by his family. When she queried them with him he didn't know what they were for.

I wanted to reserve judgement and hoped they were just helping him make purchases or manage his money, but it was starting to seem as though he may have been viewed as a burden and a cash cow, the former possibly being used to justify the latter.

I'd had personal experience of family members asking if it was worth getting my brother Christmas or birthday presents. He doesn't know it's his birthday they would justify, and what does he even need or want? See also that Conservative MP who during the 2019 election hustings posted a theory that learning disabled people should be paid less than the minimum wage. The non-person mentality, they are worthless and ergo worth less. If his family were strapped, they may well have figured that taking from him was like stealing from nobody, and that they needed it more, they had bills to pay, and they had cared for him, and bought him stuff, and other excuses and justifications besides. I tried not to draw conclusions too early, I hadn't even met them, but my protective streak towards the learning disabled had been awakened and I was wary of these people.

When I phoned the brother-in-law back to arrange a meeting at Mark's flat, his friendly voice – one that had eased in tension since the first call, which had resolved the stressful matter of the funeral, and was therefore possibly more truly him this time – seemed at odds with the picture that was painted by the stories I'd heard.

Unless he was a very good actor, my instincts told me that this was a nice guy. He spoke kindly about Mark, said that he was sweet, sometimes lost his temper and got worked up, confided that he found those outbursts hard. I told him that my brother had tantrums too.

In my mind I was remembering the time he got over-tired and I took him for a drive to amuse him, his favourite thing to do. He spent the whole treat moaning and when we got home he refused to take his muddy boots off and pushed past me, running around the house stomping mud all over our white carpet whilst shouting, 'shit, shit, shit'. I expect the brother-in-law was recalling a similar example in his own mind's eye because at the very same moment we both said, 'Yeah, they can't help it, they get frustrated' then laughed and said 'snap'. He seemed to have an understanding and a sympathy, so I dialled down the judgement until I could meet him and see the whites of his eyes.

With Steve still away, I roped in our other Community Warden Chris for the house visit. Coincidentally he had a live case on the same road as Mark's supported living flat. A giant pile of horse manure blocking a public footpath, which he photographed me in front of, for scale. A manure photoshoot and death, what a morning.

When we arrived at Mark's flat the brother-in-law was standing outside in the rain, wearing a thin coat over a ratty jumper and transporting his possessions in a carrier bag, a thinning single-use one, not even one of your ten pence jobs. He had come forty minutes on the bus to let us in. He told us he made the trip regularly to visit Mark. Added that his wife was too upset to come. She had also been too upset to visit him at the home when he was dying too. So far so completely at odds with hawking his body to medical science, and yet it had happened. Once inside it didn't take us long to walk around, there were only three rooms so the 'search' took no time. Whilst we went through a drawer which helpfully contained all of his paperwork – in colour-coded binders, obviously the handiwork of a helpful key worker – the brother-in-law went to the bedroom and picked up a remote-controlled car, one of the many toy cars littering the flat.

'Could this be placed on his coffin, please? It was his favourite one, we bought it for him last Christmas.'

Muddled by the fond last wish contrasted against what I had heard, we left the flat with the paperwork and the car, which I tested out back in the office, driving it towards people's desks and pondering out loud to them the idea of sitting at the back of the chapel, controller in hand, driving it in behind the coffin. I decided against suggesting it, in case it would cause offence, but I suspected, knowing my own brother's sense of fun, that Mark may have loved the idea.

I then phoned the priest of choice to see if he would be up for doing a freebie for his congregation member. Not only was he happy to do the council service for free, but he told me that he was also going to host a second service for nothing where the ashes would be scattered at the church Mark had requested with the full choir in attendance to sing his favourite hymns. After the initial suspicions and aspersions, this case was taking a turn for the better.

The free priest also offset the cost of moving the body, a terrible thing to have to consider, but I had a budget to balance; my least favourite part of the job. Thankfully the next task was to drop a cremation certificate and remote-control car to Lisa, one of the arrangers at the funeral director, on my way to the supermarket – that was more like it. Then, as the priest and the family knew what they wanted the service to look like, I stepped back into the administrative shadows until the day-of, though with plenty of small moments of contemplation about my own brother and my feelings about our respective endings to keep me ticking over.

When the day of the funeral came around I arrived at the crematorium early and saw the brother-in-law sitting on a stone bench in the memorial garden. Same thin coat, same ratty jumper, same threadbare carrier bag. He was clearly very poorly off. The initial tone of our call, which I had taken as slightly cold, grasping and concerned purely with money, and which had been compounded by the follow-up conversations with carers and the bank, suddenly made sense. He was in abject poverty, not just poorly off, and he had been terrified about the cost of the funeral.

I didn't know the ins and outs of the cheques and the direct debits, though he clearly wasn't going to Vegas with the money so I duly dismissed it all. The medical science incident, I concluded, would have definitely come from a place of fear, a last-ditch attempt to avoid being thrown into huge funeral-related debt. They didn't want to hand Mark off, they just felt they had no choice, I hoped anyway.

And I think I was right. As we entered the waiting area together, the priest was there with the sister. It was the first time I had met her, so I extended a hand and asked how she was doing with everything.

'Not well at all,' she said, crying, before grabbing the

extended hand and bringing me in for a hug. The priest explained that she had been in denial that Mark was dying to the point where she didn't want to visit and see the truth of the matter. She'd reluctantly made one last visit the week before he died and then had a final phone call the day before.

'You told him you loved him, he told you he loved you and that was all that mattered,' said the priest as she leaned into him and he put a supportive arm around her. 'We've been keeping her busy though,' he said to me, 'she's been helping me run the half-term club at church. We're doing a circus theme this year, the whole place is done out like a big top with me dressed as a ringmaster.'

'That's a coincidence,' I said, 'I went to a church in your town a few months ago to ask about a family grave and the place was done out like a spaceship with the priest dressed as a Jedi.'

'That was me,' he said grinning, 'Pleased to meet you again.' I laughed and apologised for not realising. 'I didn't recognise you without your beard and cape,' I said. Smallest of small worlds we agreed, before putting on our game faces and heading into the chapel.

The true funeral would be the scattering of his ashes the following week, so it was just the sister, brother-in-law, priest and myself for this one. The coffin was carried in to the Dambusters theme, remote-control car sitting proudly on top. At this they both turned around to face me, smiled and gave the double thumbs up for the enacting of their wishes. I double thumbs-upped back, which felt wrong at a funeral, but they started it.

Mark

Aside from Dambusters, the service was one hundred per cent religious with nothing of Mark, so I didn't cry as I had expected to – even from a selfish place of working through my own stuff and having a potential dress rehearsal of sorts – as I am a total heathen, so there was very little to connect to, beyond his little car which sat there as a visual reminder of him throughout. Though the funeral wasn't for me, to be fair, it seemed to be just what his sister needed. Her faith was clearly important to her, as I took it that Mark's must have been to him. They had all gone to church together every Sunday so it bonded them, and she gratefully received the many assurances from her priest that Mark was now safely in heaven with their mum and dad.

Her deep and emphatic nod when he said this made me wonder if it was more than her belief that she was affirming. There was a mixture of extreme grief and also peace in her demeanour when he said the word 'safe', the very thing I wanted for my brother, by counter-intuitively wishing him dead before me. Did her peace of mind and my peace of mind come down to the same thing; having our brothers safe from harm, either with God or in the great nothingness, but either way, not left behind, alone?

As I watched her convulse again with sobs after that moment had passed, I resolved that the price of this peace of mind would have to be carrying the grief. This would hopefully ease it though, by transforming it into an active rather than passive situation which I was at the mercy of. A good way to frame any loss really: the other person is saved from the pain of losing you and you're carrying the grief for you both, saving them. Of course, I thought to myself, you could always croak first, yeah well, if that happens it happens, I snapped back at myself, and the great thing about being dead is I can't worry about anything anymore. Whilst it seems funny to write the sentence 'the great thing about being dead', dead is actually the ultimate neutral. When you think about it, a good deal of being alive is worse than being dead by bent of falling below the neutral line into annoying, boring, or painful, like a jammed printer, spreadsheets and migraines respectively, so there's a strange part of me that is quite looking forward to it, in time.

Then came the hymns, which were thankfully led by the priest who had the voice of what I later learned to be an ex-opera singer, so he covered up for my complete ignorance of the pace and tune. As we filed out, I decided not to ask the question about conflicted feelings around grief and relief, it would have been selfish, so I just said goodbye and watched them walk towards the bus stop arm in arm. I thanked the priest for an excellent service and for giving of his time for free.

'Thank you too,' he said. 'You helped them so much, you made them feel safe.'

My hunch was correct, they had been scared. The grateful phone calls that followed to both myself and the department, along with a thank you card that subsequently arrived, all spoke to huge relief and appreciation. Something that further reinforced my attachment to the role. It seemed to strengthen slightly with every case, every person I had the opportunity to rediscover, or whose family I was in a position to help. I picked up Mark's car and handed it back to Jodie who would return it to the family with the ashes when they were ready to collect them in time for Mark's funeral II, redux.

Sadly the brother-in-law died six months later. Unfortunately he died in a hospital out of my area so I was unable to take his funeral on and the council in the district where he died refused to help, on what grounds I have no idea, leading to his wife having to take out credit. She told me that some of his last words were 'get Evie, she's my favourite' which I made a mental note to raise in my end of year review; became someone's dying wish, objective exceeded.

As usual the most emotional part of the job was immediately followed by the least; it was paperwork time. I raised and took an invoice to a branch of Mark's bank the next day on the off-chance he had any funds left. We often do these funerals in default but run an invoice by the estate to see if any of our costs can be recouped. We also look for valuable items when searching, in case anything can be covered that way. It's something I always hope to avoid, but as one next of kin said: 'Don't worry, it's unpleasant but totally necessary.'

With no money left in her relative's estate, after a very salubrious start in life, I ended up hawking his car for scrap value and taking some small heirlooms to a house clearance company, such is the rate at which life can unravel. The guy doubled his offer when I told him it was for a Section 46, saying 'for his funeral kitty' as he produced some extra notes and folded them into my hand. The instant empathy and the kindnesses that these cases provoke constantly reassure me about the goodness of most people, their instant compassion for the dead meaning that nobody is left behind at the end. Though we probably need to tap into that energy for the living a bit more, revering them as well as the dead, and not just talking fondly of them once they've gone and can't hear us anymore.

I sprinted to the bank in the pelting rain, wearing Ali's coat as I hadn't brought one. It had been glorious sun to start with but had descended into one of those days where the sunshine and the rain tag-team each other. The rain had stopped by the time I emerged and I walked back to the office, breathing in one of my favourite smells, that impossible to describe scent of wet air cut through with sunlight. Glad that the family cared about him, sad that they had been so cornered by their financial situation, and happy to have concluded the case and more or less closed the book on my own feelings before I went home for the week.

But as I arrived back and went to put my out-of-office on, there it was, an email from the coroner with another referral. The sun and the rain weren't the only thing tag-teaming it seemed. I phoned back saying I could certainly take the case on and asked for the details to be emailed across so I could get started. I was prevented from working overtime however by the death report not coming through. After the call, I waited. I refreshed my inbox. I phoned IT to see if it was caught in a firewall. I then phoned the coroner ten minutes after our initial call to ask for a re-send and found their offices shut for the day. No details, no way of doing anything. It was just as well though, as I actually had plans for my days off.

A friend from London was sitting locally for the cat of a famous person who was off abroad. I know, the circles I move in. We had plans to go for lunch and do some sightseeing. When I arrived at midday, the celebrity cat had gone AWOL, so an hour was spent wandering the countryside, jangling keys and calling his name. Lunch time was put back to three o'clock, it was boiling hot, and the place we were visiting was very hilly.

As I walked up the first incline of the day, I felt my pain condition flare up for what I sensed would be a big one. My head went light, then fuzzy, then the stabbing pains began. It's a peculiar beast, like being knifed and kicked by an invisible assailant from all angles. My legs burned on the way up some stairs, as though I had just run a marathon, then as we walked back down them something happened that only occurs during a really bad spell. Extreme pain shot through both thighs and my legs buckled completely. I was no longer able to do stairs for the rest of the day, unless I went down backwards or sideways, which was a problem as we were visiting a castle with lots of towers and turrets.

We made the best of it though and I stayed at the bottom playing Arthur King of the Britons to my friend's rude French knight. 'Your mother was a hamster and your father smelt of elderberries,' was shouted down at me as I took reconstruction photos of the scene from the ground.

By early evening my head was truly gone so I had to go home, pulling over briefly to throw up in front of some disinterested sheep, drug myself, and go to bed in order to enact the rest of my weekend plans which involved being away

Friday into Saturday and being around small children for most of that time. My friend's kids, not just random ones, I should add.

Needless to say, by Monday morning I was practically vibrating with pain and out of it on meds; the perfect conditions for a full search of a very cluttered house. Thanks Edward, if that's even your real name.

Edward aka Adam

The death report was in and my desk was covered in contrasting festive 40th birthday balloons which Cathy had spent the previous night blowing up after hours, along with prepping a cake and gifts. Not something I could have pictured happening at my previous job where my line manager was, quite correctly, nicknamed 'the silent assassin', something that came out at an appeal hearing where my case against him and the CEO was upheld before I quit anyway; I think I'll make the next book about that job.

After a present-opening session and some cake, I sent my reply to the coroner, remarking to Hayley, an apprentice I was training after Ali moved teams, that writing this email on a computer with balloons sellotaped to both sides of the screen felt comically disrespectful. Steve was still off, so was missing out on all the funeral action, but whilst I started the case he was dropping off a tree at my front door which he had somehow transported from the garden centre in his car. A birthday gift that would likely outlive me, perfect for my mortality-laden world view. In his absence I scooped up Community Warden Dan again who was going on leave that afternoon and was well up for a job that wasn't in his own workload, which he couldn't progress before home time without starting things he wouldn't possibly finish. Everyone seemed to enjoy a house search too. It was sometimes grimy, but always interesting.

Our first stop was the police station to fetch the house keys, wallet and a cool £235 in cash therein. This referral was most certainly not due to a lack of funds, it was a lack of family. The police report stated that there was no evidence of next of kin in the home, which was an obvious single occupancy. They had recovered a mobile phone with no contacts saved and an address book from 1997. I started to wonder if it was going to be worth booking Martin. If there was nobody present, I could perhaps say a few words. I'd sat at the back often enough that I had started to pick up on the delivery and rhythms of funeral speech. I then reprimanded myself for giving up before I had even started. Just look at what happened with Carl. Nobody had nobody. I was to be proven thankfully right on that, in the biggest way.

Edward's house was a Victorian mid-terrace that was in very decent repair and upon entering there was nothing in the way of death smell. He had been found quite quickly by neighbours. Evidently, he had friends or community ties at least. There was none of the usual build-up of post either, for the same reason, so it was rather like entering the home of a living person who had just popped out for milk and would be back in five minutes. This was in many ways more unsettling than the houses with obvious evidence of death and decay; this set-up edged death too close to normal life for comfort. The 'death can't get me in my freshly-hoovered semi' scenario. It also felt extra intrusive.

The narrow hall had a coat rack running along the length of it with shoes and boots lining the floor underneath the various jackets and walking sticks hanging up. At the end, a dog's lead was hanging on an old-fashioned looking peg with a dog's head for the hook and the words 'walk time' above it in italics. I had been wondering how long it would take for there to be a case with an animal left behind. Although there was just a lead, no sign of a bowl or food. It's odd the things that get you. I was fairly matter-of-fact about the pet, possibly because it activated the problem-solving part of my brain, going straight as it did to planning a call to a local kennels. It was the shoes that affected me more, some smart ones placed deliberately and neatly and some muddy ones laying in the position they had landed in when they were kicked off after a long walk, possibly his last one.

There was a doorway off the hall which led to a sitting and dining room, which in turn led to the kitchen. First things first we cleared out the fridge freezer, removing with some difficulty a frozen duck which had expired a decade earlier and was entombed in ice on the freezer ceiling and then turned it off. There was a huge amount of tinned food in the pantry, all in date, so we decided to load it into the car to take to a local food bank. At this point a neighbour appeared at the front door. The coroner had told him about the referral and he had been expecting us. I asked what he knew of this chap, Edward. Well, for starters, whilst his name was Edward, he went by his middle name Adam. The neighbour said that Adam had lived in the house for more than fifty years. His wife had died a decade ago – she probably bought that frozen duck, I randomly thought in my pain-induced stupor – but he stayed busy, resolved to carry on, and threw himself into his local community and his hobby. Model railways.

We had noticed this hobby already. It was hard not to. Framed train pictures on every wall, train calendars, stacks of train DVDs all around the TV, folders which I had initially hoped would contain important documents, all trains. It was becoming a running joke as we rummaged for a bank statement or a will and every time we found something that looked official or promising there came the wearied cry of 'nope, it's just pictures of trains again'.

The dining room was given over to a workbench with three metres of wood balanced on it and a tiny train track running the entire length. A soldering iron rested in the last position it was left, a pot of glue was open with a brush perched on it. He had clearly been working on this to the very last. Montaigne's 'I want death to find me planting my cabbages' came to mind. I hoped all of this signalled a quick and sudden demise, the best kind.

An entire bedroom upstairs had been turned into a display area with a highly detailed model running around the edges of the room. Hundreds of boxes of engines, miniature trees, shrubs, fence posts, buildings, people and cows lined the shelves above it on the walls. He had taken the door, which originally opened inwards, off its hinges to allow entry directly inside the model. One of the panels lifted like a drawbridge and then, when placed back down the track, connected up and the trains could run around and around the person controlling them. 'He did all of the woodwork on that,' the neighbour told us, proudly, and the electrics. He was very skilled.

I asked about the dog. Long dead, he confirmed. The lead was there purely as a memory. He and Isabel, his wife, had loved to take him for walks together. He directed us to knock at the door of Adam's immediate neighbour, the key holder, who knew him better, and who had the unfortunate task of finding and reporting him dead after noticing that his bedroom light had been left on into the small hours. The quick demise I had hoped for was confirmed by her. He had been found face down on his bed, having expired just as he was pulling the duvet back to get in. So tantalisingly close to the gold standard of dying peacefully in his sleep there. Next best thing though.

She was still visibly in shock, and not just from having discovered a body. He was healthy, active, just back from a railway holiday abroad, how could he be dead? She spoke about him in the same way as the first neighbour had, with pride. She told us about his time in the RAF and how he had often shown her a picture of his younger self in uniform. Had we found it? Could she have it? We had seen two copies, along with a squadron photo and a training handbook, and saw no harm in giving this lady a sentimental item, so Dan ran to the car and fished one out of the evidence bag. Her eyes filled up looking at it. We would definitely need Martin. I don't know why I had ever doubted we would, probably pain and meds overpowering my usual energy for the job. Reinvigorated, I took her phone number and that of the other neighbour and left happy in the knowledge that I had a couple of ready-made mourners. And also fairly confident that there would be more to come from the model railway community, making a note to self to hit them up later on the forums where they would inevitably be chatting about rare engine types.

Back in the office there was some post in my pigeonhole. No pigeons this time, but still a chance to make a joke to the room. An envelope I had sent internally marked 'Finance' had been returned undeliverable from France. Yes, the country of France, with the words 'defaut d'acces ou d'addressage' written on it. No shit, it was the wrong address. Incredibly, the misreading of Finance as France with no other location details had not stopped it from getting across the channel. Goodness knows who the postman had decided to hand it to. The first Frenchman they had seen in Calais, presumably. Putting my bemusement to one side, I wrote Finance in block caps, put it back into the internal post and made a start on my usual admin.

I made some phone calls to the mostly dead numbers in his nineties address book. Three connected, a couple of train suppliers, one long retired, and an MOT garage. I was still stuck on no family and a couple of neighbours. I would definitely need the train nerds. Sorry Adam, just messing.

At home that evening, I pushed through the grogginess

and found myself emailing, posting to, and direct messaging local railway clubs into the night. Cathy kept telling me to claim this time back, but I never did, partly because I wasn't working, I was doing someone a favour, it was personal, not business. It was also interesting, and an opportunity to meet many more people than I otherwise might. I have accumulated online friends, open offers for cups of tea whenever I am in the area, and email pen pals. For a job related to death, it has hugely enriched my life. Oh, and partly because if I claimed those hours back I'd never be in the office again.

By midnight I had found a close friend of his, a Twitter feed with videos of his trains in action, one club offering half a dozen attendees, all in turn offering to pass the word on to yet more clubs he had mixed with. In the train videos, his voice was audible, I had never heard one of my people speak before, it gave me chills. I now had a healthy amount of mourners and plenty for the eulogy which was all very nice, but I really needed to try and track any remaining family.

He had lived in the same small town nearly all his life. Any connections he had would be there, or at least findable through someone living there. So in the early hours I sent an invitation to join a Facebook news group for his area. Once accepted, I stopped short of posting to their page as it wasn't your usual 'child's bike for sale' type status, and duly messaged an admin to ask permission to request information about a deceased person and publicise their funeral. They went one better and wrote me an article which they put on their local news page.

The next day I went to a neighbouring town to register his

death. My usual registrar was ill and our local once a week satellite office in the town library was closed. It struck me that the first person I was registering by hopping a train was old train-loving Adam. Then when I arrived at the registry office, I was seated under the number from a vintage steam train, the type he would have spent his weekends chasing. Significance, I thought to myself, a total construct, but still magic when we sense it, superstitious chimps that we are. I can believe in nothing and yet simultaneously feel that Adam is with me due to some train memorabilia in a town hall seating area. I had found this to be true of most cases. I would see the person in the world around me for the duration, and after. I noticed chrysanthemums at every turn during Carl's case. I still think of him now when I see them at a garden centre or in a flower bed. I pass Conor's local pub and park outside Jean's care home whenever I go to book a funeral. I recently had an ice cream cone for breakfast just because I felt like it and thought of her as I indulged in this anarchic eating behaviour. Strange to think they never knew me but they have become a part of my life. Stranger to think that I have a job where I effectively collect ghosts.

Upon my return to the office, I was inundated with phone messages from the news piece. Locals who always saw him around, his regular chip shop owner who was going to give the staff the morning off for his funeral, and two sisters who had taken him on as an adoptive granddad. They, like everyone I posed the necessary question to, couldn't afford a private funeral, so it remained with me. One of them asked me about the council process, what it meant, how it worked.

I explained the technicalities as briefly as possible, the legal requirement, the legislation, I wanted to get past the business end of things, as I always do anyway, but also because I could hear her voice tensing up whilst she processed the surreal idea that somebody she loved had become a task on someone's desk.

Her voice relaxed as I moved swiftly on to the service, to the work that was going on to try and locate family, his will, and to ensure the funeral was fully attended. She started crying and thanked me for caring about him. In my tired and woozy state this obviously set me off and I blubbed my 'you're welcomes'. I didn't feel embarrassed for once though, the whole office was invested in Adam's story, having fielded the numerous calls coming in that morning, and were as swept along in his story as I was. This guy had a far reach, even in death. He is my prime example when people talk with pity about council funeral cases. How many of us will have the posthumous power to close chip shops? He doesn't need sympathy.

I had been hoping to roll in my second invoicing attempt on Mark's estate with my trip to register Adam that day. We had actually got a part payment from one of Mark's bank accounts, so I had made another invoice request for his second one. The second bank didn't have a branch in our town, but it did have one where I had been going that morning. Unfortunately, I didn't have an invoice given to me until that afternoon, and the next day was my day off, so not wanting to delay the return of the estate to the family any longer than necessary, I blurred the lines once more, took it home with me and decided to make a day of it. Drop the invoice, then wander around the shops, galleries and beaches of the next town. Part of the reason I always tell Cathy I can't calculate the overtime. I'm sometimes having a day out and an ice cream when I'm doing this stuff. It's not clear cut.

The following day when I went into the branch, which was a long way from where the account was held and mainly operated from, I was surprised to see the face of the man at the desk drop as he read my paperwork before exclaiming 'Oh no, not Mark.'

'Wait, how do you know Mark?'

He explained that he used to work in that local branch and that Mark had come in every Friday to collect his money and would give everyone in there a hug. All of the women in the branch would be heartbroken when he told them. Again, smallest of small worlds, and more heartening proof of the vapour trail we leave even after we're long gone. This job principally concerned with death just kept providing me with most of my more life-affirming moments.

When I was next back in the office, I wrote a letter to the sister and brother-in-law, informing them of my progress with the finances, and passing on this anecdote about their much loved brother. When I got home that night I scanned Adam's pride-and-joy photo and set up an RAF Benevolent Fund memorial page for him, publicising the funeral date, hoping to tap into that part of his life too. Then another friend of his got in touch through the news site saying she was going to arrange RAF flowers. As lovely as this case was turning out to be though, the admin still needed attending to, and I was behind in one major area: last will and testament. I'd given up on family, with nobody stepping forward and nobody he knew being aware of anyone, I had drawn a line under that, but it left me with a house full of stuff, a car parked outside, bank accounts full of money and no idea who to give any of them to. Moreover I'd had people calling in and alluding to wishes he had articulated which he had told them were set out in his will.

So it definitely existed and I needed to find it. If it was in the house, it hadn't been in any of the obvious places so I scheduled a second visit, with Steve this time, getting the band back together, and in the interim I phoned every single local solicitor, surmising from his lack of computer that he would have been the kind of guy to do it in person locally. Nobody had it.

This slight problem was tempered by some rather large progress when the council customer service line put a call to me at home from none other than the husband of a cousin, with connections to four other cousins still living. Just as I'd given up. Watched pots and all that. They didn't have a great deal of contact, indeed none of them were in his address book, and they mainly saw him at funerals. This theme looked set to continue as they offered to travel the hundred miles to attend his. Everyone besides was dead, they told me. Parents, aunts, uncles. Adam was an only child, his wife was an only child, they met and married late and never had children. The only family he had left were his distant cousins. I rang off relieved that if I didn't find the will, they could apply for probate and the estate could be handed over.

I still wanted to get my hands on that paperwork though. I had been told that he wanted his trains to go to very specific places and his money to go to charity. I wanted those wishes enacted for him.

Steve and I went back the next day. The mission: to find the will, to measure his railways so whichever group collected them brought a big enough van, to bag his jumpers and coats for the homeless drive which he supported in life, to pick him out a funeral outfit, find his best mate's spare house key, and clear out his car so that the finance company could collect it. His immediate neighbour was heading out to post a letter and we chatted briefly about what we were there to do, then she wished us luck and carried on her way. I haven't lost my great storytelling chops, you'll see why I included this apparently pointless detail later. Car emptied and best mate's spare key recovered from the glove box, we filled four black sacks with clothes and put them in Steve's boot, then selected his funeral outfit, as requested by his friends who always saw him in a smart shirt, smart trousers, cardigan, all blue. We then did the train layout measurements and finally faced down the main task.

His two-up, two-down actually had a third level which he had cut a hole in the ceiling and built a staircase up to. This staircase was covered in boxes which needed to be moved before an attempt to get up there could be made. Something there had not been time for on the first visit. As it was uncharted, I was fairly convinced all of the important papers would be up there. The hole he had made was covered in plywood that could be pushed up. As we ascended we found ourselves in a Willy Wonka-esque attic workshop with a piece of train track coming out of the wall above our heads and a train sign in front of us telling passengers not to alight.

It was magical, but also as I found out later, dangerous and completely without planning permission, having to be fixed before the house could be eventually sold. It was also ultimately very disappointing for our purposes.

We poked around and as the magic of the scene wore off the now traditional 'nope, just trains again' was weakly uttered at every turn before we went back downstairs dejected. It had been our last hope. Bedrooms one and two had been searched to death, nothing in the bathroom, nothing in the kitchen, and nothing in the lounge diner, well, on first appearances anyway. We had been through every pile of paper we could lay our hands on and opened every accessible cupboard and drawer to no avail. But that was the key word, accessible. He had clearly, upon his wife's death, turned the sitting room into a workshop. All of the furniture from his previous life with her, that would have been arranged neatly throughout the room was piled and squashed up against the wall behind his workbench.

I went in, under the bench and through some chair legs then, combining our tall and shortness, I contorted myself into tiny gaps and Steve leaned in to lift away the occasional tables and chairs I passed to him that were blocking drawer sets, that were in turn blocking cupboards. I finally got to the back and opened one cupboard previously blocked shut by three different pieces of furniture, and there it was.

At this point the doorbell rang. It was the immediate neighbour we had seen earlier accompanied by another woman whom she introduced as her sister, a spiritualist who, she told us, was a little bit psychic. I avoided Steve's gaze as I had at Matthew's funeral because I knew he was trying to catch my eye and pull a face.

The sister informed us that she had been sensing Adam's frustration with us through the walls. I fully turned away from Steve at this point. Adam was annoyed that we couldn't find something. Could that something be a will, perhaps? I had to bite my tongue off in an effort not to point out what an obvious cold reading this was given her sister being told that exact thing an hour earlier, then waved the will at them from behind furniture mountain, like I was surrendering in a war, and said that he should be happy now in that case.

When they had gone we were able to make eye contact once more and let out the laugh we had been holding in, although I must admit to warily looking over my shoulder for a minute there before saying, 'You weren't really pissed off with us, were you Adam? I mean, to be fair, you did put it behind most of Furniture Village' before momentarily shuddering at the thought of all my other people watching me go through their drawers and smalls and heckling me. The lure of ghost stories is strong, even if you aren't fully paid-up. Lisa at the funeral directors was told by a psychic that she had ghosts following her around, possibly of people who had been in storage with her and followed her home from work. She didn't quite believe it, but that somehow didn't help. My non-belief was the same. Coexisting with, speaking to people who weren't there, sensing them, all things that could be put down to trying to connect with the case and putting together the person as I went along, but which got naturally overlaid with mysticism because, let's face it, humans prefer stories to facts.

We dropped Adam's clothes at the homeless drive, his outfit at the funeral director, where Lisa and Jodie were having one of their community coffee mornings – lucky for me, as the impromptu cake I swiped turned out to be the only food I would have time for that day – and returned to the office to find that the phone number on the will was out of service, naturally. Luckily Google saved the day as usual and I tracked down the newly incorporated law firm along with the man who had originally drafted the document. The trains, tracks, books and DVDs were to go to myriad subsets of various railway clubs, the money and the estate to cancer charities. Probably what took his wife, I thought, this sad thought followed immediately by happiness at his wishes being enacted and helping others affected by it.

It was Wednesday afternoon, his last wishes were in place, everything was set for his funeral and I was about to go home. So obviously I got another referral, but he deserves his own chapter, so let's stick with Adam for the time being, and head off to his funeral for now.

The day-of, I snapped awake at four o'clock and gave up on sleep half an hour later, my brain having whirred into chatty action, and passing that crucial tipping point where it was too late to be turned back off. I wasn't excited per se, not least because that would be weird, but something like anticipation had stirred me. This case had gone from nothing to everything. I had felt my way through all of the previous cases, adding to my knowledge and research methods, and it had culminated in all of the people Adam knew meeting in one place to bring together all of the strands of his life one last time. And no chips would be served in his hometown until the honours had been done. I felt confident I could replicate this result time and again now, although maybe not the chips thing, though wouldn't that be a great new tradition for mourning someone?

I got dressed and realised I was running out of funeral looks. Note to self, I sleepily slurred, need to buy more black. I've since done this by the way, gradually snapping up any nice black dress I see in a sale and creating a funeral section in my wardrobe. Feeling restless and wanting to force a start to the day, I found myself at Adam's house by half past six. I was ok to go alone now, the first searches having been carried out with others present, so no valuables unaccounted for. It was still dark, the sun just starting to peek over the horizon and outline his furniture with a low glow. The darkness inside the house, along with the heavy silence, made the place feel both strangely empty and yet full of him. This made sense, I supposed, fifty-odd years of living there, he was practically in the very walls.

The silence felt like a loaded precursor to him, actually speaking to me. It was heavy, expectant, every time I turned around I felt him behind me. I laughed at my own unease at this ghost that I felt flanked by on all sides and jabbered nervously, to myself, in the form of a conversation with him, just to fill the pregnant air with something pedestrian and grounding.

'Feels like I'm being watched, Adam. Sorry for rifling through your stuff again mate, it's just you've cousins coming from a long way away, and I figured they would be the best people to take the family snaps. Excited for your funeral? There's quite a few people coming, you'll be pleased to hear.' And so on and on and on. The co-codamol in my system may also have been a factor.

I finished separating the family photos from the train ones, the latter group outmatching the former by ten to one, and loaded them into my trusty bag for life, but more often death, the amount of funeral errands it was put to. I put the train pictures in a big pile for his model railway friends to take, as set out in the will, and left the house one last time. Before I did, I stopped and turned to say goodbye and tell the energy around me, that was almost certainly my own tiredness mixed with coffee, pain, meds and sentiment, that it had been an absolute pleasure, mate.

Due to my dawn antics I arrived at the crematorium obscenely early. It was my first funeral at the new council-run venue, built in the fields which I had recently discovered Adam used to play in when he was a child. I pictured him there as a boy, I didn't need to imagine it, I had seen the photos that same morning. I visualised him running through the wild flowers and then fading and turning to the dust that would be scattered days later in the same place. A reminder, as if I needed it, that we were all due to return to nothing one day, the indifferent landscape around us forgetting we were ever part of it. An idea that sounds morose at first but that I actually quite like; life goes on without you, relax and enjoy your turn, then disappear as mysteriously as you came.

I walked around the grounds for a bit to clear my head. Bee-friendly flowers had been seeded and everything around the building was buzzing with them and beautifully wild, except for the calm, clear lines of the contrasting zen garden and water feature that ran alongside the glass window of the chapel, throwing ripples onto the ceiling on sunny days, hypnotic circles on the surface when it rained. If you were going to be turned to dust, this was as nice a place as any.

I had been there for a visit a few weeks before and had the backstage tour. I went behind the curtain, literally, the one that closes on the deceased, and peered out of the door through which the coffin is rolled after the service. The door can only be opened when the CCTV shows an empty chapel and the light goes green, to avoid anyone from the backstage area ending up staring out at startled mourners. I went through to the viewing room where families can press the button to send their relative into the cremation machine, and then out the other side to look into the incinerator itself which was in full 1800 Fahrenheit flame. A few bones from the almost completed job were still visible.

As I peered through the glass viewing hole, the worker told me that sometimes the cremation process made the body sit up, another fun fact, this job was full of them. The viewing hole was surrounded by a circle of metal and the red glow through the glass in the middle made it rather look like Hal from 2001 or the T-1000's eyes in Terminator 2 when it was missing its human suit. From there, I was taken to the room where the ashes were filtered through a giant sieve and anything that hadn't burned up – coffin handles, screws, hip joints and fillings – were put into buckets for recycling. I looked down at two buckets full of various add-ons to long-gone humans, about as arresting a moment as you will get. As I headed off, they were about to cremate the brain of a car crash victim whose body had been burned some time earlier but whose brain had only just returned from the inquest. Never a normal day for me, not anymore.

Martin arrived soon after I did, wanting to check the music and do a run-through, followed closely behind by Steve who was on his way to another job but liked to attend where he could. I showed them Adam's photos that I'd retrieved that morning, and the crematorium staff gathered to look too and ask questions about this man. From the funeral director through to the person who presses the button, in my experience, everyone cares about the individual they are dealing with and are eager to know all about them. I hope that knowing this will give some pre-emptive comfort to anyone worried about ending up as a council case. We always use the phrase 'taken into our care' instead of 'collecting a body' and not just as a euphemism to take the sting out of the words, but because that is exactly what is happening.

Cars started to arrive and the waiting area gradually filled. People whom I had only spoken to on the phone or online gradually became real and hugs and handshakes preceded chats about everything that had happened between us, and about the man himself. I tried to do a head count but, with everyone milling around, and with so many people to talk to, I gave up. A colleague from Comms had heard about my funeral cases, how they often came good, and had come along to write one up as a positive news story. She estimated fifty, not bad for someone who had a mobile phone with no contacts in it on day one.

The hearse arrived and I was delighted to see the jumper we had taken from his house on that second visit draped on top. Trains all over it, knitted by his late wife. Next to this were the RAF-themed flowers with little plastic spitfires sticking out of them. The three main aspects of his life represented: Isabel, trains, and his time in service.

He was carried in to the extremely jaunty sounds of the 'RAF March Past', which raised a few smiles and made me feel like saluting his coffin. Martin's eulogy, having been informed by so many people, was brimming with stories and facts. The whole thing felt like a family funeral, to the point where one of his friends even stood up to deliver a short eulogy of their own. I was so busy listening and watching people's reactions to their personal stories being mentioned that I didn't have time to feel sad. Until afterwards, when his adoptive family came to find me and thank me through sobs. Being hugged by crying people, impossible to remain stoic. I was getting gradually better at this though, and after a couple of tears I gulped it back down, eyes still wet but game face on.

'Do you want his jumper?' I asked. Of course they did. So remembering the route from my tour, I waved my security pass at the door leading into the cremation room and asked the attendant if he could pull the coffin through so I could grab it. He checked the CCTV and when the chapel was cleared and the light went green, he opened the door and through Adam rolled. I took the jumper, patted the coffin, said 'bye, mate' and ran back out to find them, now chatting to others in the funeral party outside. They were all due to head off to a nearby café for a wake organised by the cousins, whom I handed over the photos to. I told them I was sorry not to be able to come. It's a frustrating gear change, I explained, from all of this to an office, a jammed printer, and a meeting about stats.

Gradually everyone left and it was just myself, Martin, Steve and the Comms colleague remaining. It was her first time attending a council funeral and her articulation of it was like listening to my own first experience. The coffin, the service, everything felt so strangely proper. She didn't expect to feel sad about someone she didn't know, but it was really affecting. That's the power of our stories. From zero to a connection in a fifteen-minute re-telling. She could see how, after my many weeks of building this picture, I found the job so consuming.

She headed off and Steve, Martin and I, joined by Jodie, had a quick catch-up in the sunshine. We had become a tight-knit group, bonded through the work we did, bringing each other out of the heaviness of the funeral afterwards; back to life.

Back at my desk, I emailed photos of the RAF flowers to those who couldn't make it, then signed everything over to the solicitor who was thankfully also co-executor of the will.

The other executor having developed advanced dementia. Adam's wishes would be enacted and his track layouts would continue to be displayed around the country by his friends, who subsequently told me that the one we had seen in his bedroom had been modelled on the area where he had been deployed in World War II. Meanwhile, his RAF bomber servicing training book sat on my desk, with his annotations all over it. I emailed a few museums to see if we couldn't also make sure Adam became history too.

And then I turned to my next case which had come in just days earlier and would stand in stark contrast to Adam's. It would also teach me a lesson about acceptance. I had always pushed for attendees or a complete story, for me that was the mark of a successful outcome. I would have to redefine success in this case and learn to let go. Here's Alex.

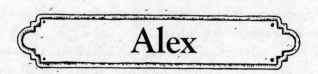

Alex

This case started as it meant to go on, messy. It immediately threw me, coming as it did from a funeral home – the point that usually lay beyond referrals, which typically came when a body was still in the morgue or coroner's office. It threw me to the point where I didn't even recognise it as one at first, due to its also being couched as a casual plea for advice.

They had picked up a body in the early hours from a care home and the family who had come in that morning didn't have any money. Any. At all. This rather begged the question, what was the body doing with them then? Who had instructed them?

They told me how, after learning of the financial circumstances, they had offered the family – a son and his wife – the cheapest package they had; a direct cremation on credit, to be paid off over a year. Despite this working out at under one hundred pounds a month, they still couldn't afford it.

They then asked if I had any ideas. This is probably the bit that threw me. I wasn't usually asked in vague terms for suggestions about private funeral arrangements, which is what I fully assumed it was if they had already been instructed. They gave me the son's number, suggesting I could talk to him about things. Vaguer still.

When I got through I realised that advice was not what they were calling me for. They were trying to push me towards him so that either he could self-refer or I could offer to take him on. Advice was code for, 'we've been lumbered with a body and, oh dear, we're not getting paid, you take it'. Why they didn't come out and say that I don't know, we're all in the death business here, perhaps they thought it crass. Luckily, the son's desperate tone tipped me off from the get-go and after establishing that he was one of an ever-growing group – the working poor – who would not qualify for DWP assistance, I took him straight on.

And there began one of my most spartan, disconnected and unsatisfying cases: my first unattended funeral. An outcome I could not even fight to rectify, despite having access to his family, or rather because of it. It just wasn't my place to overturn their wishes, which was to have no service for them to attend, to just cremate. I couldn't pry beyond what little they wanted to tell me. I had no individual agency to place a story in the local paper, which wouldn't have been appropriate anyway for a person whose identity and connections were fully known. There was no house for me to search either – he had died in palliative care after having stayed in his son's spare room for a short while following a near lifetime spent abroad – so no clues to help me seek out friends or fellow hobbyists and probably none to be found in this country anyhow, nor any objects and items to glean personality and passions from. To ask the son for details of people who would be willing to attend would be to indirectly accuse him of letting his father down by not going himself.

Ultimately, I had to respect boundaries and know that he would have had his reasons, good ones too, no doubt; it would take quite something for a son to swerve his father's funeral. Similarly, I didn't want to judge the dead guy either, who couldn't speak for himself. It might have been six of one. It could have been completely one-sided. It didn't matter now, anyway. It was over.

Success in this case wasn't going to be a full chapel or brimming eulogy, but a quick and quiet end to a fraught situation. No service, no need to try and force poems and readings which didn't mean anything. To feel bad about not feeling bad. To feel abnormal compared to other 'normal' families. As if they aren't rarer than the dysfunctionals.

Elective relationships are imperfect enough but families are forced together in a quite terrifying manner. If someone told you tomorrow that there was a big tombola machine full of the names of everyone in the world, and whoever was drawn would be made to live with you for a minimum of sixteen years, you would be rightly fearful of what kind of interloper would be entering your home and life. Can I trust them? Will we get along? Hold complementary beliefs and lifestyle choices? Are they unbalanced, dangerous, cruel? Well, that's how our parents and children are selected for us, a cosmic tombola. We have to make the best of it, and if we can't, then this.

As we worked through the referral sheet, I got some glimpses of a family that had been fractured. Marital status elicited the information that whilst Dad was technically married to his mum, they didn't speak anymore. 'Put 'estranged',' he said. We stayed well within the lines of the form, so I only learned the name, Alex, his date of birth, GP, the fact that he was a retired university lecturer, and that the living arrangements – raised during an enquiry about his possessions and the house search – were an attempt at rebuilding a bond. I could only guess that the marriage had broken down, likely due to Dad's behaviour, and that the children had gone with Mum, physically and emotionally. Alex, heading off abroad, compounded an emotional distance by laying a few thousand physical miles on top of it. Perhaps realising he was near the end, he wanted to return home, build bridges. It sounded, from the dejected tones when describing this, as though it had all come too late.

Despite not wanting a service, there was grief in the son's voice, probably of the complex nature. I had a couple of months prior gone on that bereavement training I had made a mental note of in Conor's living room and in parallel, had witnessed a friend struggle with the death of an abusive parent. No grief is typical, but where there's been trauma, it becomes overlaid with relief which can fuel guilt. Unfinished business and unresolved anger continue to fester with no hope of resolution now. Sometimes the self needs to be completely redefined after a lifetime of being rooted as standing in opposition to the parent. And whilst 'normal' families mourn what they had, fractured families tend to mourn never having had it, and no chance of ever having it again either.

My enduring memory from the training though, as instructive as it was, was the moment just before we broke for lunch when the trainer asked: 'So, is everyone happy with traumatic death?' Well, yes, but you know, obviously, no. Odd to think that I now have a certificate that says I understand the grieving process. As if it's something you can actually know. The individual and lonely experience of grief, check. Like claiming to have a doctorate in pixies. Everyone was there for a different reason, some were nurses, hospice workers, one random heir hunter looking to hawk their card around, and then there was me and Steve. When we went around the room and they asked about our aims for the day, we told them about the role, how it usually ended up with us being the ones to break the news, often via the deceased's own phone, their number displaying at the other end, and then our unfamiliar voice kicking in, saying that they were dead.

'How do you deal with that?' she asked, coming out of trainer mode, genuinely interested.

I paused and thought about it properly for probably the first time. 'Acknowledge it's weird,' came my answer, simplistic but true in its instinctiveness. It honestly helps to just lay it out for what it is and say, this is weird, for us both, let's say it and then we can get through this hard conversation together. She made that the mantra for the day in the end. Death.

Acknowledge it's weird. Put that on one of those lame hanging signs that usually says 'Wine O'Clock' and I might actually buy it. Actually, I don't need one, my downstairs loo is already adorned with a cross-stitched home sweet home-style hanging which says 'life is pointless and everything dies'. My taxidermy partner made it for me and I always forget it's there and get funny looks from tradesmen who use that toilet when on a job.

But back to the son, whose grief sent me off on this tangent. I told him I would attend the crematorium and see his dad off and then let him know when the ashes were available. He almost cried with relief when it was all confirmed. The debt he was facing down that morning lifted from his shoulders. His life could resume. His wife was nine months pregnant and they were broke, he needed to focus on that. His gratitude was almost too much to handle. Every other word a 'thank you'. A grovelling 'thank you'. Peppered with apologies for taking up our time and funding. For his dad only having £1.37 in the bank and no estate. Offering me his dad's Nutribullet as part payment at one point. Or perhaps his own time to help the council out in future. It wasn't heart-warming gratitude though, it was self-flagellation, it was uncomfortable.

I assured him no apologies or thanks were needed, that this was what we were here for. I hated that he felt the need to prostrate himself like this. He had a job, was working hard, had done nothing wrong, but the unfairness of the system had robbed him of his right to dignity. It reminded me of a family I had dealt with who, upon meeting me at the crematorium,

opened with 'so sorry about this, we always pay our way...'
Not something they should have felt compelled to say on the
day of their uncle's funeral. I had plenty of time to put them
at ease though, as the hearse was stuck in a tailback and
the guy was half an hour late to his own service. This also
lightened the mood as they joked that he would have been
the same in life and that they would have words with him
when he finally showed up. Both myself and the priest had
screeched across the grass central reservation to escape the
same jam he was stuck in and take the back roads. Possibly
my most action-packed start to a cremation. Obviously not
something a hearse could pull off though, so we had to leave
him for dust. Pun kind of intended.

I called the funeral director back and informed them that
I would be taking Alex on under Section 46 – subtext, you
can unbunch your knickers now chaps – and they breathed
a confirmatory sigh of relief. Although the matter of the
fee for the removal of the body remained an issue. They
asked if the council would be paying for this. I turned off
my dulcet funeral tones and activated my business voice –
the faux authority I had cultivated during Angela's case had
become real – giving a hard 'no' to that. Explaining that
we weren't even aware of this guy's existence when – and I
paraphrase now – you were busy smuggling him out of the
care home bed in the wee hours per your blatant informal
arrangements to take all their dead, so that they could get the
room ready for another customer by sun-up.

If anyone owes this money, I told them, it's the care home
who, according to my spreadsheet, had been told about

looking before they leap already. I took mercy on them and agreed to be the one to break the bad news, then staying in business mode and, weaponising my no-lunch-break-today hungry grumpiness with a side of burgeoning headache, I called the home with my spreadsheet open and the exact date they were contacted about not moving bodies until funeral funding was established on screen. I informed a very angry matron type that the person who called it in pays the fee and reminded her of our letter. She deemed our rules ridiculous, refused to pay and demanded to speak to my manager, so I gave her to Steve who isn't my manager but who's to know, and he put on a very convincing boss voice and carried on the argument whilst I phoned the GP. In so doing, I stumbled into the next administrative disaster.

In their haste at wanting rid of Alex's body, the home had not called out a doctor to declare him dead or to sign off on the cause. Six days had passed since his demise. The Shipman law working well there. The GP was surprised to hear that his patient, whom he hadn't seen for months, was nearly a week dead. I explained what he already knew, that no medical cause of death meant no registration was possible, and asked if he could possibly remedy that today as the five-day window for registration was already closed.

Even though none of this was his problem, he kindly agreed to duck out of a very busy surgery and walk down the road to the nearby funeral home – the only positive about the body being in the wrong place – to declare somebody who had been in a body bag for six days, to be dead. Perhaps the most existentially pointless errand anyone on earth would do that day. I called the funeral home back to tell them to sit on him a bit longer until the doctor came and stood down our guys from going to fetch him right away.

I then got on with some other work – issuing a taxi driver with plate number 666 as it was Halloween and too good of an opportunity to miss – whilst eating some pity crisps Hayley had chucked at me and waiting for the call to come through about the certificate, which arrived last thing. Perfect, pick it up first thing in the morning and take it to the registration appointment I had speculatively made in a spirit of pure hope for the following afternoon.

When I arrived at the register office the next day, a biker wedding was just finishing up. Confetti was being thrown to the sound of roaring engines. I had ten minutes before my appointment so watched them take their photos and then waved the bride off as she jumped on the back of her groom's Harley, the motorcade noisily following them away. A reminder that the nicer stages of life also pass through the register office. Births, marriages, not just what I was there for. The death made official, I texted the son to let him know and told him that I would inform him of the cremation date and time once booked so he could at least stop and observe the moment at home.

As I didn't want to prolong the agony I went to the funeral directors the following morning, on my day off. I was going that way anyway, en route to the garden centre with my mum in tow. 'It's bring your mum to work day,' I explained to them as I wandered in. Well, bring your mum to your non-working day anyhow.

As we walked round to the sofas, I asked them if they had seen their competitor's shop window display opposite and then filled them in on the very unusual placement of the elf on the shelf on a selection of coffins, which we all agreed was odd, even for us hardened deathlings.

We had done these forms dozens of times so Lisa and I chatted in the margins as I signed and initialled away. Mum told her all about me as a child, as mums are wont to do. How I had always been preoccupied with death, written horror stories aged five, the baby bucket list, followed by my brief funeral director ambition at age six. I had apparently picked this up from walking past a funeral home on the way to primary school each day. She told them how, on one occasion, I had turned to her and said, 'Did you know that they put lipstick on dead people in there?' Kids say the funniest and most disturbing things.

My death awareness had started way before that though. I had great grandparents who were stumbling towards the finishing line during my very early years. When I was around three or four, I asked my great grandma how old she was. She informed me that she was 99 and I replied, 'Hmm, you're going to die soon then aren't you?' She laughed and agreed that she probably would, yes.

My mum had asked me on the way home, whilst admonishing me for being so blunt, how I knew about all that. Probably the osmosis I mentioned in my introduction, Wile E. Coyote falling off a cliff or something, but it was also something that I had observed myself. I told her that people got wrinkled as they got old, and then they died, like when fruit goes shrivelled and has to be thrown away. What an analogy. She also told Lisa something I didn't remember myself. How, in addition to the traditional old shoe box, I had made her wrap dead pets and random birds that expired in our garden in her best towels before they went in their coffins, to give them a proper funeral. Serious foreshadowing. I chimed in to say that, to be fair, I had been made to sleep in a bedroom every half-term at my nan's where bodies of dead family members had historically been kept for viewing, with black and white pictures of these severe Victorian relatives staring at me from the walls, so any strangeness was down to conditioning, thank you.

Jodie popped her head around the door to join in, and to also tell Lisa not to eat the Jelly Babies in the desk drawer as they were to go inside Mr so and so's coffin. Mum looked at me as if to say, is this a normal day for you people then? I looked back as if to say, you don't know the half of it. As there were no requests about specific dates, or indeed anything, it took a lot less time than usual and so we sat there for half a minute at the end, the process feeling strangely incomplete. Very much in keeping with the whole feel of the case.

On the drive back, Mum said not to bother with all those arrangements for her, all that money. We'll see, I said. It would be a little bit off if I put loads of effort into say, Adam, and then none into you. Though I did share the exact same sentiment for myself, but again, would those left behind stick to it? Would it be unhelpful to them if they did? Funerals are for the living and the deceased not wanting a fuss might not work for those left behind who perhaps needed to work things through.

As he had come up, we talked a bit about Adam. She asked if I had ever found any family. Just cousins, I confirmed. It's a shame he didn't have kids, she said, before asking if it had made me want children, so I didn't end up like that. Well, I said, Alex has a wife and children and he currently has nobody attending his lack of a funeral. Families aren't a guarantee that you won't have an empty chapel. Families can also be found and made elsewhere, like all of Adam's friends and connections. Though I was certain that Alex would have connections out there somewhere, it just wasn't my place to seek them out, so it's an irrelevant measure really, the amount of people in a specific room on a set date.

I texted the son the cremation date for his information, now becoming aware that in addition to never learning anything about Alex, I would never get to meet his son either, the way I usually did at the culmination of every other case. The whole thing was shot through with disconnection like a stick of rock, even from my perspective. He replied to tell me that his wife was due to give birth around that time. How symbolic, I thought, a second chance at a father-child relationship brought into being, whilst the first abortive one was being incinerated and put to rest.

And that was it, nothing else to do. It was like a phantom limb, I perpetually felt like I should have been doing something, per a normal case, but there was nothing. Well, except fielding emails from the initial funeral director who were still banging on about the body removal fee, due to the care home digging their heels in and refusing to pay.

They were mostly in contact with my pretend manager

Steve, who was doing a great job of frustrating them, with me in cc.

I came back from my days off to see that they had requested the son's contact details so that they could chase him for the payment instead. Despite referring him to us due to his known inability to pay for a direct cremation over a whole year in the first place, nice. Steve refused, citing data protection, which was useful cover for the baseline reason of it being amoral to chase someone mired in debt because the organisation who owes the money is being belligerent. Also, what was a couple of hundred quid to them when they clearly had a lucrative deal with this home that churned them deceased people aplenty. Just tread more carefully next time. After all, we're in a world where one in one hundred funerals is now a Section 46.

The week before his committal, the crematorium emailed to ask me if I had any music suggestions for playing Alex into the chapel. I hadn't booked a service at the son's request, and direct cremations usually enter through the tradesman's entrance, but the crematorium manager had no services booked at that time and so decided it would be nice to bring him through the front door and play him in while we did.

I phoned the son but there was no answer, so I fired off a text, no answer, and then an email, ditto that. As we started to edge towards the weekend I still had nothing, so I emailed the crematorium to tell them to play whatever they saw fit, feeling disappointed that even with a family contact there would be no personalisation. Then on the Friday night, as I was sitting in bed coincidentally writing up the beginnings of Alex's story in my diary, Steve messaged me with a link to the song that the son had contacted him that day to request. It was a religious song, sung by a gospel choir, very affecting. As I sat there, listening to it, staring off, getting goosebumps, it turned out Steve was doing exactly the same thing at home too. He messaged me on the Monday morning asking if he could come tomorrow, having felt slightly haunted by it all weekend.

I had already made myself a bouquet on the Sunday out of the verbena and roses in my garden, but now I needed another, so the morning of the funeral I went out in the pouring rain and made one up for Steve from lavender drying in my shed and three sunflowers that I cut and tied around the base of the spray with gardening string. Looks artisan, I thought to myself. Twenty quid for that in London, I bet. The bag for life and also death got another airing for floral tribute transportation purposes and I set out for the office in the atmospheric driving rain to do some desk work before the service.

'I HAVE NO BIN AND NO ANSWERS' was the very existential heading of the first email of the day. As tempted as I was to reply suggesting this as a possible title for the movie of their life, I referred it to Waste and got on with some actual work. Next up was an email entitled 'Poo gate' which had bonus photos of said poo and 'of the man who done the poo outside our house' attached. This job really did encompass everything from the sublime to the repugnant. When I went to look on our system, a case history for their address popped up. 'Wants advice on a duck race' was the title of the last service request they'd made. They had it all going on at this place.

The office windows were rattling as the storm rolled closer and every time I looked up from the inbox of the weird, the contrasting gloomy conditions outside had worsened. Heavy wind was causing the rain to sheet sideways, smashing water against the glass with force, so much of it that it blurred the view completely. It felt like Alex's angry and mournful spirit was having one last strop. Have at it fella, I thought, then realised my inner monologue was addressing condensed moisture falling from clouds, or maybe myself, it's all processing isn't it?

As I got up to leave, a wave of laughter was gradually spreading through the office that sent me off into the dour conditions, on two levels, with a nice reminder that life is daft. An all-staff email had been sent entitled 'FW: Message from KM_C458' because whoever sent it had done so straight from the scanner. This is urgent, gibberish title be damned. The text of the email said, 'Has anyone seen my lovely mug?' and the attached scan was of an actual drawing that they had done of it, not hastily with a biro, but with some degree of detail and in colour, so there were colouring pencils involved. The words 'missing mug' had been written above the sketch making it look like a really tame Wild West 'wanted' poster. No doubt a stream of all-staff emails saying you shouldn't use all staff email for this would follow. Those are worse than the original infraction guys, don't do it.

Steve and I set off with plenty of time to spare given the choppy conditions, and drove through the eye of the storm, chatting here and there but both feeling quite muted. When we arrived at the crematorium, the car park was starkly empty. We ran through the rain into the equally empty waiting area. The loneliness of the scene was imposing. No Martin pottering about checking the sound system. Nobody to meet or greet. Nobody. Well, except us, always us.

The hearse arrived and Jodie got out and ran ahead of us to ask what the plan was. After all, this was a direct cremation, just through the front door rather than the back. We explained that there was some music cued up for our entrance and that a crematorium staff member had been moved to devise a mini-service, just a few words before firing up the cremation machine, to acknowledge the person.

Jodie ran back and started the traditional slow walk in front of the hearse to the chapel door. Rain lashed the car, and poor Jodie, and it was too windy to place flowers on the coffin for the carrying-in as they would have been carried away. Instead we followed the coffin, spine-chilling song filling the chapel in full surround sound, and placed the homemade flowers when it was set down.

Despite knowing nothing of this man, I gulped down a couple of tears as I placed my flowers. Jodie, who usually leaves the chapel for the service, sat down next to Steve and I to listen to the poem and words of committal that were read out by the volunteer crematorium staff member who had brought a smart change of clothes to work that morning especially to perform the impromptu service, as he usually wore a polo shirt and shorts for his work out the back in the cremation room. Then the song started up again as we walked through the side door to meet his coffin coming through from the other side.

As there was nothing else to do, no mourners to talk to or celebrant to debrief with, we watched the machine fire up and waved him in, my flowers and all. Steve also used the time to have a mini-version of the tour I'd had weeks earlier. As we drove back to the office, the rain cleared and the sun came out. It was as though the whole sorry situation had been put to rest, exorcised. Maybe Alex was trying to tell us that he was grateful for the impromptu funeral. Or maybe a new weather system was coming in. You decide.

It wasn't all doom and gloom though. As I arrived back at my desk and fired off an email to the son describing the morning's events and enclosing photos of the flowers, a phone call came through to Hayley.

We have a sort of code when taking difficult calls, usually expressed through mimes or pained cross-eyed facial contortions and she was giving me both the wild eyes and the pantomime shrug of futility. I hadn't actually noticed she was on a call, as the person on the other end hadn't afforded her much chance to speak. When she finally got the case reference number out of them she was able to see that they had not responded to our request to complete nuisance diaries per our procedure, accordingly the case was closed pending their return.

At this point, Hayley moved the phone away from her ear as the voice at the end started to resemble an irate cartoon caller. She handled it though, followed the protocol and said that the diaries once returned would prompt the case to go to an officer for investigation, and no, no we can't just come straight out, no, sorry, no. The person unable to circumvent procedure angrily hung up, or rather tried to. They smashed the phone down but missed the receiver and Hayley sat there listening to them stomping around the house saying what a disgrace we were.

'Can I hang up now, if they think the call is over?'

'Oh for sure, you could have hung up when they started shouting at you to be honest.'

When showing her how to make a record on the case file, I looked at the details over her shoulder. It was the old woman who smashed into my car and didn't apologise because these things happen. Sounded like she could stand to take some of her own advice when it came to her noisy neighbour situation. Coincidentally, or significantly depending on your bent, the noise source that was winding her up was from model railways. I hoped my man Adam would have been proud that his hobby was part of my sort of revenge. Maybe he had gone so far as to haunt her for me, by way of a thank you.

On a less schadenfreude-laden happy note, I received an affirmative response from a museum in Adam's town to my email offering his RAF book for their collection. I dropped it off during a food shopping errand, my life and death admin so often intermingled, and as I signed it over and gave the details of the original owner, someone having a browse at the back end of the museum shouted 'Adam? Oh I knew him!' Of course they did.

A demonstration of just how fitting it was for this popular

local figure to end up there as part of the town's permanent history.

Adam's story rounded off nicely, Alex's out of reach, but surely out there somewhere. I took solace in the fact that they both got the maximum that it was possible for me to give them and accepted that those degrees would vary from case to case.

I received a hugely grateful email from the son, thanking me for being there with his dad at the end. His happiness at a service of sorts taking place, of flowers being placed on his coffin, seemed to speak to his not feeling able to attend, rather than not wanting anything at all, and retrospectively changed the sad complexion of things. He thanked me for going above and beyond, not that I had done all that much in this case compared to some, but the feeling of personal responsibility for each life I was handed was impossible to shake.

It was sometimes a heavy weight to carry, albeit entirely self-imposed, but I couldn't turn it off, it was a reflex, so I was stuck with it, but glad of it. I was still grateful, however, for a slight break from the emotional grind when a different kind of case came in, an exhumation.

An Exhumation and a Tea Break

Time for a shorter chapter, an intermission, to give you a breather as I know from personal experience that the funerals can get a bit much. I can only apologise that my idea of a breather is talking you through an exhumation. Nature of the job, nature of weird old me. But at least it's the opposite of a funeral and I think that's what we all need right now. Plus, it's an even more little known part of the role that deserves an honourable mention.

We had a request come in shortly after Alex's funeral.

'Put one to rest, get another one straight back out – balance,' said Steve as he showed me the instructions and licence for the next day. Neither of us had done one of these before, they are mercifully rare, with most people ending up in the correct grave in the first place, and then hopefully being left there forever after. Though sometimes people do take their dead with them when they relocate – like the forty-two nuns one of our colleagues had to oversee the exhumation of when the nunnery moved premises – and occasionally there are mix-ups, like the one we'd nearly had to do a month prior concerning a man who had been buried with his brother, before a family member who knew them better pointed out that they had hated each other all their lives and urged that they be separated, even though further rows were, at this point, fairly unlikely.

We were primed and ready to attend but got stood down at the last minute when the gravedigger devised a clever plan, based on the soil type, to dig down to the coffin, then tunnel through to the next plot and push him into the neighbouring grave sideways. The chap never came above ground, so it didn't count as an exhumation, and ergo no Ministry of Justice paperwork or Environmental Health assistance was required, slick. The soil in this latest case, however, was solid clay so the old letterbox drop technique would not be possible.

It was a pre-dawn start, so as to reduce the amount of people who could wander by and potentially witness the scene. The location was a rural churchyard perched high up in the hills above the shoreline of a seaside village edging along our area, in open and sparsely populated countryside. The weather that morning, yet more driving rain and high wind, combined with the darkness of the still night-time sky to evoke the archetypal horror movie backdrop befitting the reopening of a grave.

I pulled into the car park in front of the church, a wonky old building surrounded by wonky old gravestones, most of them truly ancient, the churchyard dating back to the 1100s. I turned off my engine, then my lights, and sat there in the pitch blackness trying not to nod off. I had slept appallingly and given up at around three in the morning. Breakfast eaten – if you can call a Tracker at 3.45 breakfast, it's nearer to a midnight snack – and with nothing else to do at that time of the day, I had set off far too early and arrived first by some distance. After a while, bored with sitting in the car, I wandered around in the pitch blackness with only a few churchyard up-lighters, illuminating the rain drops into pillars of bright white swirling water, to guide my way.

I stood in the middle of the graves and monuments, representing all of these lives I would never see into, took a moment to consider how each one of them might have meant something to me had I met them or had them as a referral, how many people I would never meet or know, how many people I know but don't see enough of, how you needed a thousand lifetimes to befriend and love everyone it was possible for you to connect with; also pondered how weird my job was, always sending me off on some philosophical tangent, filling my heart and mind with sadness, joy, love, loss, a sense of disconnection and a sense of unity usually all in one go, and then found the plot in question. Recce completed, I hurried back to the car because, however boring it was just sitting there, I needed to seek shelter from the rain until everyone else arrived rather than catching my death and needing to be chucked down the newly-dug hole as well later on.

The person we were relocating had been in the ground for a week, to the day in fact, but unfortunately the wrong bit. In a series of events fit for an old-fashioned farce, the mason had removed the wrong headstone in preparation for the re-opening of the grave, namely that of the one next door, an already fully-occupied family plot. This first mistake triggered the second one; the gravedigger taking the missing headstone as his cue, then dug up this incorrect plot instead of the neighbouring one where the deceased's husband had been patiently waiting for her for twenty years. Stonemason cock-up notwithstanding, the gravedigger should have known something was up when he reached the very limited depth left available to him in what was very obviously a full house. But for whatever reason – needing to get to another job, chips for tea, something good on the telly – he had just buried her in a shallow grave, patted the soil down as hard as he could and gone on his way.

There was, incredibly, a small mercy to be found in all of this: the deceased hadn't been bunged in with strangers. The neighbouring plot belonged to the same family and she was now having a sleepover with both of her in-laws. I am aware that there's every chance she's heckling me as I type this, like Adam via the psychic, and saying no, this was in no way fortuitous, you never met them, but what I mean to say is that it was considerably better than ending up with randoms because, in addition to the obvious distressing reasons, this scenario would also have involved tracking down and dragging another family into the fiasco, which would have in turn added a few weeks or even months to the paperwork side of things. This way, same family, one signature, one time, bosh.

I sat in the car looking out onto the dark country lane that had seen no action since one tractor had gone past half an hour before, when I suddenly saw a set of headlights snaking along it. The car slowed as it approached the church and swung in from the road, stopping right next to me in the car park. Ignition turned off, the interior light came on, and I could see the occupant, a middle-aged man in a suit.

We tentatively studied each other from the safety of our respective vehicles for a moment, just in case the other wasn't actually there for this exhumation and were coincidentally parked up for something more nefarious. A bit of loaded eye contact and a knowing nod later and we got out for an introductory chat.

He was from the funeral directors who had been instructed with the burial and was sufficiently devastated about it all, even though it wasn't in any way his fault. Personal responsibility for the deceased, comfortingly ever-present. He fetched a golf umbrella from his boot for us to stand under, but it was of limited use, the rain was blowing in sideways. As we were smacked in the face by water and wind I attempted small talk, but he was miles away, fidgeting from foot to foot, fixated on the horizon he himself had just emerged from. He was clearly willing the sight of the set of headlamps that would hail the arrival of his saviours; the gravediggers who would be putting everything right and allowing him to sleep again after a week of worry.

Sure enough, after a short while, the vista lit up and over the brow of the hill they came in a white van that screeched into the car park, chucking up the gravel. Out they jumped, two young cheery guys who spent the rest of their working lives doing roofing and labouring with this niche area topping up their income. Hot on their heels came three pallbearers who would be helping to lift the coffin they had not long since placed.

Steve was still en route, so we walked down to the grave with me taking the council role until he arrived. Environmental Health have to attend these to ensure public health and decency are maintained. As we arrived at the grave everyone looked to me for the nod and, fake it 'til you make it, I who knew nothing about this until the day before, put on my best official voice and instructed them to please put up a gazebo first for discretion. Which they did; the power! Well, it was more a collection of tarps from the back of the van tied together and held up manually, but they did the trick. Steve then arrived with the paperwork and assumed the main officialdom role as I took photos and made notes for the case file from the slight shelter offered by a giant statue of Jesus with his arms outstretched. Thank you, oh Lord.

Improvised discretion gazebo in place and passing dog walkers shielded from the Burke and Hare tableau, the digging began. One of the guys did the exhuming whilst the other dug the correct plot to the legal depth. It didn't take long for the first guy to reach the coffin, it was only half a spade's length down; a tenacious fox could have got at it if they had wanted to. I took a case file snap of the gravedigger posing with his shovel to show the depth, or lack thereof, then retreated back underneath good old Jesus.

Despite being a shallow grave, the wet, compacted clay was hugging the coffin hard and it took two hours to free it. First digging down to reveal the top and then digging around the sides until the handles could be grasped and a lift could be attempted. Even after such a short time in the ground, the coffin lid had caved slightly in the middle under the weight of the soil. 'Oak veneer,' said one of the gravediggers, tapping it. 'You see this a lot, people think they're getting solid oak but it's a con.' The funeral director said nothing on that point.

The coffin was ready to be lifted just as the final shovel load of soil was thrown over the other digger's shoulder. These guys obviously worked in rhythm. As the dirt landed, something rolled free from it, stopping right at my feet. I remarked to Steve that it looked like a skull. Well, crikey. It looked like a skull, he replied, mostly because it was a skull. Presumably that of the husband. One person's dignified repatriation had become another's post-mortem decapitation.

After twenty years in the ground, the husband's coffin was long gone and his fragmented skeleton resembled those unearthed during archaeological digs, or something you would see on a pirate ride at Disney. This somehow made it familiar and impersonal, and strangely easier to face than the ghosts of the people I dealt with but never saw outside of their coffins. We pointed out the rogue remains and the gravedigger reached his shovel out from the grave, scooped it up as respectfully as one can pick up a skull with a spade, and placed it gently back inside with him. Husband returned to his rightful place, it was time for the wife to be returned to hers.

The gravediggers and bearers fed the webbing under and around the coffin, then lifted sideways, and lowered.

The process was complete. Well, almost. The family would be coming back later that day for a second blessing and a caved-in lid would not be a welcome sight as they gazed down into the grave for their second last goodbye. The bearers went to their van and came back with a brand new lid which was placed on top of the compromised one, new brass plaque and all. As I looked down into the grave and took my final photo of the successful outcome, it was as though she had just this moment been buried, with none of the dramas I had witnessed. A satisfying if strange way to end my working week.

This strangeness continued into my non-working days as I found myself the next morning sitting in the tea room of a London museum getting ready to talk about death with some strangers. The reason for my busman's holiday was that my friend, the one with whom I had attempted taxidermy, obviously, was keen to attend a Death Café, and I was the mate most likely to. Having just come from an exhumation, I couldn't argue with her logic.

A Death Café is exactly what it sounds like, a place with tea, coffee, and sometimes cake, where people gather to talk about death. The first one was founded by a man called Jon Underwood, who posited quite correctly that 'if people thought about death more, about the fact they were going to die, then there would be less bullshit' and so out of this philosophy and his front room sprung an entire movement. They now take place worldwide and are gaining prominence and popularity. Although judging by the very few social media likes I got for my Instagram picture of the properly nice bone china with death captions and hashtags, there is still much work to be done around normalising death and bringing it into everyday life.

But why would you want to? I don't hear you cry, because you are one of the enlightened ones who buys books about death and faces it head on. But let's pretend you're not. Why dwell on something that's going to happen anyway, and waste the time you're actually alive worrying about the end? Well, to answer the question I presumptuously put in your mouth, it's not about worrying. It's about eradicating worrying through planning, control, understanding, rationalising, and then accepting. And a lot of the conversation revolved around these things, with people starting off stilted and nervous, slowly becoming more animated, then writing notes as ideas and knowledge were shared, before finally leaving with a to-do list and a lightness in their step.

We were at a table with a ninety-year-old and a four-month-old – he hadn't come alone, his owner had brought him – and I was in between them, both literally, seating-wise, and by virtue of the fact that, at forty years of age, I wasn't far off their mean average. We were like a human timeline of birth, life and near death. The new mother's reason for attending was that she was a planner and having small children, being so close to fresh life, made her think of her own death. I knew exactly what she meant. It was more than the impulse to get your will in order in case something happened to you, but something more existential. New life is the furthest thing away from death, and yet the nearest; fresh out of the nothingness to which it will one day return.

As you hold it, you ponder life and naturally death, well you do if you're weird like me. Whenever I am given a new baby to cuddle I always think, welcome to life, and also to death, you're on the clock now too with the rest of us pal.

The ninety-year-old was ready to die. Both existentially and literally. She had prepared written wishes, an end of life plan; the order was absolutely 'do not resuscitate'. Though she had been defied before by a doctor who had deemed her too physically fit to be allowed to go during a period of recent hospitalisation. She was furious about being pulled back from the brink against her will, and passionate about assisted suicide, which she said would do much to ease her worry. She had been a nurse in her youth and had seen plenty of cruelty to old people. Shouted at, hit, left to sit in their own faeces. She did not want that for herself. There was no sadness in her, she was just ready. It was the kind of death zen to which we should all aspire.

She went to these events whenever she could. Her proximity to the end making her the perfect attendee, making her relevant in a world where older people are side-lined and ignored. Here, her every word was hung upon, and her pronouncements were devoured. It reminded me of Fight Club, where he went to support groups for the terminally-ill because when people think you're dying they really listen to you. She also wanted to talk about legacy. She had no family, nobody to speak for her when she was gone. She wanted to tell her story. I thought of similarly-aged Jean, with her incomplete eulogy, and wondered if this would have been my experience of her, had we met over tea at a Death Café.

In addition to talking through our thoughts, there was a lot of useful information imparted too. Google's inactive account manager, Facebook's memorialisation settings, downloadable digital will templates, expressions of wishes forms. I got home and spent the weekend having a death spring clean. I nominated someone to take over my online accounts and wrote a digital will. I then emptied my cupboard with my papers and my handwritten note. I was about to switch energy supplier so, knowing this needed to be updated, I decided to make the note, ironically, a living document, saved on my computer, hard copy in the cupboard, to be replaced with updated versions as things changed. I also decided to revamp it and add even more detail, including minor things like the contents of my wallet, along with my top tip for getting reward points bequeathed; buy yourself a Boots meal deal on me, in the unlikely event I haven't redeemed it first.

I put my papers in categories, in different coloured folders and cross referenced them in the document. I wrote my instructions in a chatty way, made a few jokes. When I read it back I laughed and thought, 'ah, it'll be a shame when I die, I am quite fun'. So I got to mourn myself a bit too, which was a bonus. I also got to see myself the way I see my people, through admin, notes, and snippets. My life would one day be reduced to this, more or less indecipherable, lost even, but I was no less real for it, and nor were they.

Anyway, has everyone finished their tea and been to the toilet, because that's enough of an intermission. Though it's lucky we had this deathly tea break together because things are about to get very busy again. Enter Covid-19.

Donald

It started as a low key and abstract news item. The one playing out on the telly in my introduction, where death is happening elsewhere, but not to us, not today, not ever. By the time I was due to go on a ghost hunt down a disused nuclear bunker – another one in the competitive birthday gifting series – the Covid rumblings were getting nearer, like with thunder, when the pause in between claps gets shorter and you know the storm is almost overhead.

As it was, we squeaked through, and managed to attend our last social engagement for a good long while. Though the seance that night was cancelled because, even though the virus hadn't hit yet, it wasn't considered wise to join hands, just in case. Trust my first experience of social distancing to be rooted in talking to the dead.

As we unwittingly spent one last night together in a semi-recognisable world, albeit a weird one full of ghost stories and cold war memorabilia, we thankfully didn't take it for granted. The good thing about being acutely death-aware, your end is constantly in your mind, so every second counts, and you enjoy life more. Death is a great motivator and, ironically, life coach. It stops me mid-gripe and quickly reminds me that one day I'll regret wasting a single second on cross words aimed at someone I love. It will also one day save me from ever having to change a duvet cover again too, so whether I'm unharassed and dead or seizing the day and alive, death is a win-win for me really. Though the constant knowledge of it did make me permanently semi-anxious whilst writing that I would die before completing this book.

We ran around darkened rooms and tunnels, tried hard not to laugh as the medium informed us of an evil, hooded figure in the room who was angry that we were sitting in his chair. The fact that an evil, hooded figure would own an item as banal as a chair tickled us on its own, but the three bears-type outrage at people sitting in it meant we had to wander off into the darkness and take a moment. At two in the morning, I was sent into the men's to say 'was that you, do it again' to some obviously self-flushing urinals. We emerged at four in the morning giggling, exhausted and ready for a five in the morning bedtime. The next time I saw the outside world properly there would be no toilet paper left in it. I texted my ghost-hunting companion from a decimated supermarket when I got home later that day. 'We should have stayed down that there bunker,' I said, quite correctly as it turned out.

Nine days later, the storm was well overhead and I let my train to London leave without me and my hotel room for that night sit empty, as all of my plans up there fell like dominos. Nothing was official yet, lockdown wouldn't follow for another seven days, but the world was already taking responsibility for slowing itself down in the absence of government instruction, before shortly thereafter coming to an official full stop. As friends were gradually furloughed or put out of work altogether, my job was about to go in the opposite direction. And as I sat down in early March 2020 to write a risk assessment and order more PPE, I never thought I would be more prepared than the government who, weeks later, were telling funeral directors to make masks out of paper towels and bin bags. Actually, what am I saying, I could have easily guessed I would be more prepared than them.

Days into lockdown, the phone predictably rang. It was Lisa from the funeral directors with the opening gambit, 'I've got a body out the back which I think is for you'. Imagine having that sentence said to you. And then imagine it actually being pertinent. Welcome to my world.

I was at home when she called, though our offices remained open throughout and I was working there on a rota. I would go into the office for a couple of half days, or one full day out of my three, and usually find myself alone with one or two others drifting in and out. The anxiety about leaving the house was mingled with excitement at there being bog roll where I was going and also the need to get properly dressed up, which even led to me over-excitedly putting in curlers for those days. I would try to diffuse the deserted post-apocalyptic mood by seeing how many times I could spin round in my chair before getting dizzy, timing my riding of a wheelie office chair from one end of the floor to the other and, when I found out that Outlook 365 could read your emails aloud, making my computer swear at me. I would flinch when a visiting officer came in, pleased to see them on a human level, but backing away in paranoia to make a clear path past me.

Daily death toll excepted, I think my most poignant moment of the pandemic was seeing desks taped off and signs put on them saying 'do not use'. The new normal forcing us apart, the chatter of the fully-occupied office gone, no more quiz questions, no more tea thieving – no more tea rounds either, they were outlawed, the only upside, I could finally have one with no repercussions – and Hayley the apprentice having her contract immediately axed, sent home with no leaving do. The website moderator had also gone, so I could have posted a picture of Paul Daniels on the front page and nobody could have stopped me. I think it speaks to my good character that I resisted. An extract from my diary from a day during the peak sums up the mundanity amidst the atmosphere of quiet crisis: 'Only two pieces of post today, both from Covid conspiracy theorists. One was a 5g hack, the other was a little more imaginative and submitted a two-page, double-sided rant about the Catholic church and dairy. They finished by saying that they did ask the council to 'stop dairy' previously but we didn't. In many ways, we caused this pandemic.

'Had an email from a guy who is annoyed that we've pulled the lifeguards from the beach. Presumably because this has spoiled his plans to get into trouble in some water this weekend. Though why anyone would want mouth to mouth in this climate is beyond me.

'Somehow, despite there only being three people here today and the resultant reduced lunchtime odds, someone has managed to stink the kitchen and entire place out with that uniquely cabbagey office microwave stench you get. Horrible, but fondly reminded me of the before times.

'Keep having to pull my mask down to anxiety snack on Kit Kats, these are the kind of things they don't cover in the disaster movies.'

By contrast, I ate nothing at home where all routine was lost and ended up having to bulk buy Build Up to stay alive. Which brings us back to me, at home, not yet not eating properly, and taking my first lockdown referral. The man in question had been sent to the funeral director by a care home, his cause of death, bronchopneumonia. Care home dead weren't being tested so I had no way of being certain, but it seemed to scream Covid-19. Particularly as he was only 65. And particularly when, upon phoning them back days into the case, I found his carer to be off work with symptoms.

I was unable to carry out my usual searches as the improvised guidance that was being written up on a daily basis, along with common sense, put care home rooms off limits. So I phoned the home to establish what items were in his room, if there were any clues to be found in amongst them, and to get my basic referral information. Instead of sitting in the day room with a cup of tea and flicking through the care file, I stood over a laptop I had just collected from IT, that was failing to connect due to my working from home kit needing some kinks ironed out of it. In the end I had to take his details down at the bottom of a used shopping list.

It seemed very appropriate for the disconnected and chaotic times we were now in that my usually meticulous form was replaced by a scrunched-up bit of paper that said, *milk, bread, cheese, Donald Beckett, died 26/03, no next of kin.*

That scrunched-up paper was a list that I was putting together for my first online grocery shop. I had always been a free-wheeling shopper and liked to buy the food I fancied each day on the way back from work, but that wasn't a thing anymore, unless you had a death wish, so I needed to visualise what I would be buying. I remember that in my first ever delivery they had replaced the limes I had ordered with lemons, so I actually got to live out the old 'when life gives you lemons' proverb. But with life being Sainsbury's. And the lemons being literal rather than figurative. And no deep philosophical lesson, just a different tasting juice.

Everything was going online. Shopping, and comms too. I was now in three work WhatsApp groups. Some of that old office atmosphere shrunk down and made portable. A couple of tense moments when Dave messaged everyone at silly o'clock and one of the people who didn't have notifications switched off was woken up. Face-to-face contact was mostly restricted to Teams. Strangely, much more intimate in that you got to see people in their homes, spouses walking past in the background, children calling out, cats wandering across keyboards, but also far less so in that they were many miles away and personal interaction was, for the time being, a thing of the past.

But back to Donald. The lack of detail that followed added to this feeling of disconnection. The home didn't know his middle name, his marital status, his former occupation, his religion. He had no visitors, no known next of kin. The sum total of their knowledge was his name, birthday and that he liked television. Thankfully this was due to dementia. I only say thankfully in relation to such a terrible affliction because it means it wasn't due to disinterest on their part.

And so I started tackling my admin in a very different world. Doctor's surgeries had shut their doors, so medical cause of death certificates could not be picked up. The registrar had shut their doors, so appointments could not be attended. The funeral director was open, but with locked doors, and screening of all those who turned up outside. This was the one and only area where the disconnection kind of worked for me, though. Instead of driving miles around the district between the surgery, the registrar and the funeral home, I made three calls. The doctor emailed across the medical cause of death certificate, the registrar registered the death by phone and the funeral director gave me a date and posted me the order. Hopefully we can keep some of these elements when we come out the other side of this, I thought, whenever that may be. The emissions it would cut and the time and energy it would save.

I had considerably less bad pain days during this period – who would have thought a pandemic could improve your health? It showed what was possible if needs must. Though the lack of human interaction and the loss of the formality and ritual of registering, whilst convenient for a council worker, clearly wasn't ideal for mourning families and would have to be reinstated, at least in part, eventually. I asked the registrar how he was finding talking to the bereaved by phone with no eye contact or intimacy.

'Hard,' he confirmed, in a weary tone.

Admin sorted, I set about my usual searches and did what I could with no paperwork, photos or clues, just the limited information I had. I searched his name on social media, put it through Google, all to no avail. Then, dejected, I trailed off into a brief period of peculiar paralysis. Lockdown seemed to make the days slip away from me fast, whilst I concurrently felt a massive sense of contrasting inertia in my guts, wandering around slowly in those lost blurry hours as if through treacle. No meal times, just eating what I wanted, whenever the mood took me, which wasn't much and wasn't often. My old routine gone, time had no meaning. I felt like a caveman with no clocks, living instinctively, suddenly finding it had gone dark, so it must be time for bed.

I was yanked from this haze by an email from Martin, linking me to the music he had chosen for the funeral. 'The Lark Ascending'. As I listened one evening, I suddenly found myself sobbing. I think I needed a good cry anyway, and it was as good an excuse as any, but the music was so moving and I pictured myself a week or two later in an empty chapel with that song playing, and nothing much being said about this forgotten man. I had to have another go at finding out who he was and who he had once been.

I sat down that evening and Tweeted a request for information which, what with everyone in the country being at home to see it, very quickly blew up into hundreds of re-Tweets and replies, plus dozens of private messages. People with ancestry accounts came up with two possible matches for that name, both born in the same month and year, one in Scotland and one in London. I Tweeted the press for both areas and they spread the word further. Whilst Twitter did its thing, I turned to Facebook for a more local angle, applying to join a group for the town where he had lived.

Within hours I had two messages from former carers at a previous home where he had been more lucid. I learned that he used to own a motorcycle repair business, which he claimed to have bought with buried treasure; his proudest moment was riding in the motorcade at the wedding of Charles and Diana; he'd had an accident which prevented him from riding again and he had owned a dog called Socks who was so beloved that he was given his own bedroom. He was described as a great storyteller with a lovely smile and sense of humour, well spoken and very caring towards others in the home. His favourite band was Queen; out with 'The Lark Ascending' then.

They then said that he spoke of his children often, despite having not seen them for many, many years. He had family then. Had they dropped him off at a home and forgotten him? Died? Or was this a case of estrangement? The carers had no names, locations or clues so I decided to just take heart in the information I had. I sent it over to Martin and returned to Twitter to tell everyone invested in the story what this mystery man had been like in life. People replied asking for the date and time of the service so they could stop and think of him; raise a cup of tea. One local even offered to attend. Heartened that a lonely end had been transformed by the unconditional care people have for the dead, a care that assures nobody is truly alone at the end, I got into bed, content that I had achieved as much as I could in this case. As I went to set my phone alarm, I received a message. Three words. 'That's my dad'.

I waited for a follow-up message to appear underneath it, but none came, and those blunt words just sat there staring at me, hanging uneasy in the air. I replied with shaky hands, not knowing how to pitch it. Were they indifferent, were they yanking my chain, were they upset and rendered speechless? I erred on the side of the latter and apologised that they had to find out this way, explained the situation and asked if they would like to attend the funeral. I watched as the message was viewed and then waited, and waited, and waited for a reply, before giving up at one in the morning, turning off the light and sleeping fitfully.

When I stirred the next day and the memory of the previous night seeped back in, I reached straight for my phone and the reply from his daughter was there. A slew of emotion, the reasons for her estrangement from him laid out, but only as context, there was no malice or anger, just shock, weariness and at the core of it an overarching sentiment of love. She wanted to attend the funeral and we arranged a phone call for later that day. I immediately took to Twitter to stand down the kind local who had offered their presence in lieu.

Now that family had been found it would be inappropriate and moreover, as I later learned, hugely awkward, as the family dynamic went beyond estrangement from the deceased and involved estrangement between the remaining family members too. The social distancing rules, which were proving distressing at other limited services across the country, seemed made for this one.

I dialled nervously, given the emotionally-charged message, and it wasn't long before her partner had to take the phone from her as she couldn't speak for crying. I suggested I email all of the details across for her to take in at her own pace during the initial period of shock, along with Martin's details for contributing to the eulogy when she was ready to talk.

That night, in perfect symmetry with the one before, I was about to go to bed, content again that I had achieved as much as I could in this case, when I received a message. 'Think this is my dad can u call me'. As it was midnight, I messaged back and promised a call first thing, on my day off, though so often not. Then once again I slept fitfully before once again reaching for my phone the second I opened my eyes. I stayed glued to it for seven hours, eventually getting showered, dressed and eating breakfast at two in the afternoon. During that time, I spoke to the whole family.

First the sender of the message, a son, who was stricken with grief, but also a sense of peace for having learned about his father's funeral when he did, and not after the fact – which would have denied him the chance to attend and put things to rest. He spoke of how the family had split apart, his mother having left first, followed by his sister, followed by him. He had bought Socks for his dad to give him something to love in the absence of his departing family. The accident had changed his personality, made him impossible to live with. As with his sister, there was no resentment or anger, just resignation that a bad hand had ripped them all apart. And as with his sister, the overriding sentiment was one of love.

I then spoke to his sister again, who was now over the initial shock and able to talk more. She was anxious about the involvement of her brother and mother, neither of whom she wanted to have anything to do with. It was strange as, having spoken to the brother and subsequently the mother, all three of them seemed lovely people and very similar, particularly in their feelings for the deceased. They all told slightly different versions of the family story but you could see the thread of truth running through it, nobody was lying or malicious, they just saw it from a different angle, and there was a pathos in the re-telling that made me think they were all very sad about the situation.

With both of his children at odds and both wanting the ashes, I phoned Lisa next and asked if they could be split. There was a small fee for this, she told me. The council didn't fund extras, so I just went ahead and paid it myself, they needed it, and it wasn't like I was going on holiday this year or indeed anywhere much. But at least Donald could. They both wanted to take him to his favourite place. Both of them had a different notion of where this place was though. By paying to split them I would be allowing them to each have a final significant moment with their dad, and Donald had a fifty-fifty shot of ending up where he wanted to be. I also paid for the ashes of the case after Donald to be couriered to his family who couldn't leave home for the funeral, as I couldn't stomach the constant disruption to people's grief during this time. Jodie had to get her husband to bring their kitchen scales to the office to weigh the guy for the quote, another surreal moment to add to the many.

As I hung up on Lisa the next call came straight through, his ex-partner, their mother. She had been with Donald for nearly twenty years before having to leave due to ongoing arguments and then his eventual wholesale personality change. She always checked up on him though, but had suddenly lost sight of him one day when he went into the care home. Him being so young, she didn't think to look for him in such a place. The forwarding addresses she had for him all drew a blank and she had to give up. Sadly, at around the same time, Donald was asking his carers to help him find his estranged family, but his dementia meant he could not furnish them with enough details. They were on opposite sides of the looking glass, it was awful really.

She asked me when he had died and then gasped and told me that she had been washing her curtains that day and had hung them over the landing to dry, using the heavy rings to weight them down. As she lay in bed that night she heard an almighty crash as they fell over the bannister and landed downstairs.

'He always said he would come back and haunt me,' she said. 'I think that was him telling me he had died because every day since I was thinking about him and it made me search his name online. That's how I found your Tweet.' Belief or not, it was nice to see her forming one final meaningful connection to him through this story.

She shed some light on his claim about starting his business with buried treasure. They used to go metal detecting as a family and on one expedition he had found an antique gold coin that sold for many thousands. I went back and told his carers the true story behind this tale he had often regaled them with. On another expedition, they wandered into a field with an angry bull lurking in it. The family ended up hiding in a tree whilst Donald enticed the animal away with his packed lunch. We were on the phone for over an hour with happy memory after happy memory being recalled, in between moments of sad reflection on it all falling apart and leading to the current mess.

The last call was from his sister-in-law, phoning on behalf of his elderly brother, whom he hasn't seen for thirty years, and his first wife, ditto that. I had collected the entire set. None of them would be coming to the funeral because of underlying health conditions and having moved on decades ago respectively, but as with his estranged close family, he was spoken of with love, and even his first wife had been sad to hear the news. He must have been a decent guy to have stayed in the affections of people he had either had a fraught, or limited relationship with. A quick call to Martin to pull everything I had learned together – which drifted off into a brief chat about 1980s kids show Knight-mare, and the boy who panicked and told the wall monster he was in love with him during a challenge to cheer him up, because it can't be all doom and gloom – and I was finally able to have some cereal when most people were taking afternoon tea.

Donald

In the days before the funeral, anxious messages kept coming in from Donald's daughter who was fearful of facing her brother after all these years. I found myself choreographing their arrival times, so that I could stagger their entrance into the chapel and seat them one at a time on opposite sides. Their mother wasn't coming due to underlying health conditions that kept her in permanent lockdown, so I told her the order in which the songs would be played and she cued them up and held a second version of the funeral at home.

That morning I arrived at the crematorium early, alone. No Steve, who was working at home, no shared car journeys even if he hadn't been. His noticeable absence underscored the very different scene to the one I was used to. The entrance to the office was barricaded by a table and cordoned with red and white tape. This was due to someone having wandered into reception during the early days of the pandemic to request a tour of the facilities for the upcoming funeral of their relative. They only mentioned as they left that this relative, with whom they'd lived, had been the first victim of the virus in the local hospital.

So instead of going in for a cup of tea and a chat as usual, I shouted my hellos through a face mask. I couldn't enter the behind-the-scenes area to wait, even with my staff pass, so I paced around the main entrance. The room containing the memorial book was locked with a sign saying 'no entry without an appointment during Covid-19'. The waiting room too was locked, again with signs referencing Covid-19. Both doors were tied shut with the red and white tape. It was like an apocalyptic movie scene. I was very relieved when

Martin arrived, some human contact, a nice chat, the closest to a social I'd had in weeks. And would remain so. My 2020 kitchen calendar – what a waste of money that was – containing only funerals until at least August.

The daughter arrived first by some distance, as planned. From her numerous texts I had judged her to be the more nervous of the two, and the one in most need of getting settled into her surroundings in her own time, so that she could better cope with the addition of her brother when he turned up.

With no waiting area, we chatted briefly through face masks in the entrance to the hall. She was more than sad, she looked very physically fragile, her eyes a mixture of grief-stricken and scared, her shoulders slumped under an invisible heavy weight. She was anxious not only about being faced with her brother after so many years, but having to deal with it at such a traumatic event. We directed her inside and she chose a seat from the eight chairs remaining, the other ninety-two having been taken out to encourage and permit distancing.

When her brother arrived, his body language was less weary, but had its own anxious quality. He was restless and moving from foot to foot. Smiling to greet us and then dissolving into tears upon rifling through his bag for keepsakes to place on the coffin. He too was fragile. He too was scared, not wanting to enter the chapel and face his sister until he was safely behind his father's coffin as it was carried in. Jodie gave me a sad look as she passed with the bearers, sensing the atmosphere.

As instructed, he chose a seat on the opposite side of the room, not that he probably would have opted for any of the ones near his sister anyhow. As he sat down he turned his body slightly away from her, she stiffened and stared straight forward. The service began.

It was a tough gig for Martin, the two attendees frozen in anxious poses, trying to pretend they had no peripheral vision or knowledge of each other's presence. Any emotion stayed pent up as they concentrated on staring down or straight ahead and the memories didn't seem to be raising fond smiles or knowing nods as per usual. Not even the one about them all getting stuck up a tree together. At this, I myself started to get stiff and anxious, but as the service progressed and more stories flowed, they started to loosen and then cry. The son wanted to stand up and say a few words of his own but only got as far as 'Dad, I forgive you' before breaking down and being unable to continue. His anguished sobs said much more than anything he could have prepared and Martin assured him that we all knew what he meant. Thinking of it even now brings tears to my eyes. His pain was that strong, it was palpable.

The final song struck up. Donald's favourite. 'It's a Kind of Magic'. We always file out during this musical outro and the son went first, initially standing outside for a moment, before wandering slowly off towards the car park. Martin, Jodie and I stood awkwardly outside the chapel door, awaiting the exit of the daughter, and staring intently down the pathway hoping he didn't leave without speaking to her. She didn't emerge. We continued to stand there, tensely talking in low tones through face masks about what to do and having to keep repeating our muffled selves, suddenly realising that understanding speech is also in some part about lip-reading.

We assumed she was probably hiding away and hoping her brother would disperse, allowing her to come and go without exchanging a word or even a glance. She couldn't stay in there forever though, there was another funeral waiting on the other side of the entry doors and the crematorium staff would be looking to clear the room soon. As the song faded into silence, she tentatively stepped towards the exit door, our encouraging glances over the top of our face masks trying to coax her along. Her brother saw her as she came out, her body somehow even more slumped than before, looking lost and distraught.

'I wish I could hug you,' I said, as she passed me. I really meant it. Just leaving a human being standing there, stricken in that state pained me. She was paralysed by grief from the service and by the fact her brother was still in view. She stared around helplessly.

At this point her brother, now at the head of the path, turned and walked purposefully back. We watched on, glanced at each other in anticipation and hope, before collectively taking a deep breath as he stopped in front of her, silently took his backpack off and undid it. Out came handfuls of porcelain pigs, his dad's collection, which she recognised and cried at the sight of. He delicately dispensed them into a plastic bag one by one before smiling and saying 'I want you to have these.'

He held out the bag, the peace offering was there, would

she take it? As she reached out to meet him, we all exhaled and smiled to one another.

We had just seen a decade of estrangement come to an end in seconds. She fell into his arms and they hugged for several minutes. Long enough for me to sneak a photo and send it to their mother, who I had been sending pictures and videos to during the service. She couldn't believe it. They were still there when we closed the exit doors and walked around to the front of the building. They were still there when I finished catching up with Martin and Jodie and drove away. According to Jodie, who stayed for the next service, they were there for an hour and a half, making amends. Their mother texted me that afternoon to say that they had agreed to meet again after lockdown and make a go of their relationship. It was all she had ever wanted, for her kids to be together again.

In the days after, I texted them to notify that the ashes were ready. The daughter replied to say thanks and to also tell me that when she was in the chapel alone at the end, she had placed her hand on the coffin and said, 'Dad I love you, Dad I forgive you' and years of anxiety and depression had lifted. 'I'll never forget you,' she finished. This message had me crying for an entire day.

What I am about to say will sound wrong for half a second, but bear with me. They rather needed their dad to die to move forward. Their mother said the same, in my defence. The long shadow that the family breakdown, which stemmed from Donald, had cast, dissipated with his death. They could start again in this new moment. They loved him but couldn't live with him, and for as long as he lived, so too did the past trauma that kept them at odds. Now they could love his benign memory, draw a line, and finally live with each other. Death, whilst the end for some, is the beginning for others, because it has the power to change the ongoing story.

As weeks passed and other funerals came and went with people gradually getting used to the situation, offering me an elbow to bump as a greeting, sanitising their hands on the way in and out, and things feeling abnormally normal at last, I continued to get messages from the mother saying that the relationship remained on track and, as I write this, that is still the case. I also received a message from a celebrant overseeing a Section 46 service where no information was known and who, inspired by Donald's case, had done some research and come up with some facts. She said she would do this for every such case in future. Small ripples like this would hopefully become waves. These heartening moments buoyed me, but the sad strangeness of the times through which they shone like gold dust could not be easily offset. And these times also brought the toughest of cases, so any offset was even harder to achieve.

Like that of the young man with mental health problems who found everything he relied upon gone when lockdown hit. The library, café, church, community centre, everything that anchored him. He fled his house when he started hearing voices and then lived, and died, in his vehicle, leading to my first ever search of a car instead of a house, in a scrapyard, a motor graveyard where it sat silently amongst smashed-up models from serious accidents, the twisted metal making them look like they were still in chaotic motion as his remained eerily still and intact.

He kept a lockdown diary which we found in the glove box. The first entry of this period bemoaned the loss of his lifelines, the middle ones mentioned not being able to access mental health services, the last entry finished with the line: 'I feel like I am waiting to die.' The definition of an excess death.

My own lack of contact with family and friends, hugs and face-to-face chats, which were the usual outlets for my feelings, day trips and nights out to blow off steam, had weakened me. Whilst the virus stalked us and we all avoided each other and stuck to our own tiny orbits, I was left alone with the dead and my own constant anxiety about seeing them right at the end. The uptick in cases, whilst not major due to my district not having a hospital, was triple my norm and made it more difficult to find the balance I had already been so often failing to achieve. When your job is about life and death, well, life and death don't finish at five o'clock on a Wednesday, even more so during a pandemic. Messages arrive and phones ring at all hours, and you aren't going to turn down a lead because it's Saturday, are you? And what even is Saturday anymore anyway?

I resolved to look after my mental health more and so bought a zero-gravity lounger to zero gravity lounge in on the sunny days of lockdown. The chair could only be used for reading and would be dragged to the middle of the garden where my weak-ass broadband couldn't reach. The garden isn't even that big, my broadband is just very, very weak.

The hours I set aside with just a book, the sun, the wind, and the birdsong saved me and finally helped me achieve some balance. I don't think I would have found it without the trauma, just as Donald's family before me wouldn't have found peace without death.

Back at the office, the local authority cuts came in harder, despite the fact that we had been charged with a fair amount of pandemic response duties. The council were broke and so had to sell our offices and move us into the attic of the Victorian-era town hall building. The open plan team was broken up into small rooms off a long, wonky, windowless corridor that felt like walking along the inside of a pitching ship. The fire escape was through a kitchen full of combustibles. How ironic if it's my death job that eventually gets me killed. All of which made the 'I don't know why I pay my council taxes' complainants all the more annoying, and now they had an extra string to their irritating bow: 'Oh, and don't give me the Covid excuse.' Having this thrown at you for trying to explain that a lot of staff were isolating or sick was fairly demoralising in a time when one hoped we would all pull together. Someone even invoked it when I hadn't even mentioned Covid, I had actually answered their enquiry in full. I replied saying I was in an office working and replying to them, with the answer, that I hadn't mentioned Covid, which by the way was in reality affecting our employees and reminded them that a global pandemic wasn't on a par with the dog ate my homework.

The customer is not always right and the crisis made me more inclined to drop the business speak and talk on a human level. It worked, and they replied very nicely, hoping people got well soon and that the rest of us stayed safe. As time went on and most exchanges ended like this, I was hopeful despite the culture wars over masks and vaccinations that people might connect to others better and to themselves.

Might they also do this in relation to death? Talking honestly about it, planning for it? I was split on this. There seemed to be a tipping point where daily death statistics ceased to be scary and started to be numbers. The amount of people who lost their lives was impossible to picture, even if you did try and picture the enough-to-fill-Wembley-arena analogy. Individual deaths move us, one-off massacres shock us, but ongoing daily death, how do you keep up a response to that? Facing death seemed like a logical upshot of pandemic life to me, but equally logical was turning your back on it.

I did a very unscientific Twitter poll to ask if people were hearing and talking more about death due to the pandemic, outside of the factual news arena. Our survey said no, by a whisker. It was the old referendum split that keeps cropping up like a curse. The number of the beast is now surely 48/52. I had to ask because my own news feeds aren't representative, following as I do morticians, funeral directors, grief charities, hospices, Dying Matters, all of whom were churning out a lot of articles about how now was the time to face it down and positing that many would. I wasn't so sure, given how at the same time as I watched the live stream of a friend eulogising his mother in an empty chapel, many people were clamouring for beach trips and street parties and normalcy even if it killed them, literally, and others around them too. Though perhaps they were the most scared of us all, and were trying to deal with it by simply closing their eyes and wishing it gone, the time-honoured response.

Alternatively, they could have been in the cognitive dissonance camp of knowing the death rate was amongst the highest in the world, but believing that had nothing to do with them. Not to me, not today, not ever. Hopefully in the other percentile, that of those directly affected, indirectly affected or just acutely aware, a few more wills were written, a few more wishes communicated, conversations started, and unsaid things finally said. And hopefully any changes in attitude will be retained, although the human ability to return to our original position like elastic once a threat or crisis is removed should never be underestimated, especially if the original position is more comfortable. When and if the virus recedes, I expect the knowledge of death will recede with it. I came out of it all with a lovely sun lounger though, so that's something solid, and also the knowledge that I could do this already difficult job in even more difficult circumstances, so I can take anything that comes from here on.

I also came out of it with the definitive answer to my question about how my brother would cope without me should I die first. Fine, as I had hoped and suspected from his total disconnect from time, space and death. His care arrangement placed a firewall – an actual one, not a government one that involved sending people with the virus into the home – around the residents on day one of the lockdown and ceased all family visits.

My brother doesn't understand phones. He once took the handset from my mum when she had me on hands-free, kissed it because he thought I was inside it, and hung up on me in the process. Video calls he understands even less so, and just ran away when the carers attempted a Zoom. Accordingly, I didn't see or speak to him for 672 days.

I missed him, but he didn't ask after his family once, and didn't worry about my absence, assuming I was around somewhere, filing me away with all the ghost people he had known and lost, sometimes addressing me as he pushed his wheelbarrow around, like I address the soil and wind, a preview of my future deadness. And after I finally let myself cry about it six months into the pandemic, a mistake as I had a hard time stopping, I got to preview carrying the grief, whilst we were temporarily dead to one another.

His carers told me that during this period he would ride around the grounds on his bike shouting 'I am having fun.' While I was grief-stricken, he was safe and happy. As I die, I'll hold onto that thought, if I have the cognitive capacity to think it, and of course if I'm not too busy thinking something utterly banal about my trousers as I'm on board that diving plane.

I sometimes wonder what all of my people were thinking as they approached the end, and in the moment they died.

This is something I have wondered even more so with my next case than with any other, if only because it would unlock the secret of how she actually did.

Introducing… well, I don't know.

Unidentified

'There's a dog poo outside my house', said the email. What a terrible predicament, I mean, can you imagine? I replied to say that I had – reluctantly because, come on – informed the street-cleaning team. Then fifteen minutes later they replied to say it was still there. I couldn't think of what to say back, except maybe a sarcastic jab about not having sufficient staffing levels to dispatch a crack team to attend to one piece of poo immediately, and do you not have a trowel, so I deleted it. It's hard to care about such mundane gripes at the best of times, but particularly now when the more profound end of my job had just got added profundity.

Prelude, interlude, and here we finally are, at the case that was my easiest, and the case that was my hardest. Easy because there was no name, so no house to search, no fridge to empty, no hold music, no registrar visit, no invoice to raise, against no estate; just one trip to the funeral director with coroner forms to sign off a burial contract. Hard for the exact same reasons. No name, nothing doing. Leaving just the short, bleak job of burying an anonymous body, found naked and half decomposed on a beach. And all of the unsatisfying existential sadness that brings with it.

All that was known was her gender, her hair colour, her ethnic group – the unhelpfully 'broad white European' – and her rough age, the depressingly broad 25-55. No DNA or dental record matches. She was found wearing only her bra and an antique necklace, nothing else nearby. No belongings, no note, no abandoned car, no sightings of a woman in distress that night. Just an anomalous decaying body in the cold, exposed middle of nowhere; a beach at the end of a river cutting through miles of fields. A beautiful spot by all accounts, popular with walkers. When viewed from the hills above at sunset, the river becomes illuminated, resembling liquid gold flowing into a tangerine sea. Though I will never look at it the same way again. All I can see now is her body lying at the end of it.

Steve took the initial call and walked over to tell me that we had another case and to check my email. As I waited for our woefully slow internet to connect I asked him, 'Who is it?'

'Well,' he said, 'that's just it, we don't know.'

Eventually the local news link he had sent me loaded and the artist's impression of her face was staring out at me. Deep brown, penetrating eyes under the headline 'mystery woman found dead on beach'. I recognised her instantly from a year earlier when the police appeal had first launched. At the time I had quickly read the story, amongst many others whilst scrolling the site, had assumed that the usual science and enquiries would identify her and unite her remains with her family, and then moved on. But there she still was, frozen in time, unclaimed. And from the calm, steady gaze of the artist's impression, entirely unruffled by this fact.

'No need to register it,' said Steve, 'The coroner's certified her.' And off he went back to his desk. After all, this case was not a two-person job and he was off on holiday the next week. So, it was just me and her. I sat there, looking at her for a while, getting silently acquainted. Pondering how a whole year had passed and still nobody had come forward. In a six-degrees-of-separation world where everyone's nan is on Facebook, where our phones, debit cards and CCTV track our every move, a world that is getting smaller by the day, this seemed impossible, and impossibly sad.

All of that day, all of that night, and throughout the case my mind oscillated wildly from one theory about this conundrum to another. Maybe the picture just didn't look anything like her, I would think, they had next to nothing to go on. But then again, I would instantly counter, anyone with a female who had disappeared from their life would be looking at all potential missing person's stories and following absolutely anything up. They wouldn't pass her over because 'that's not Mum's exact nose shape'. Ok, so it follows then that nobody is missing her. Well, that makes no sense either as everyone has someone or, at the very least, someone who knows they exist. Especially at her age range, the prime of her life, she must have had, at the very least, a boss, a landlord, a friend. You say that, I would think in response, slowly turning into

Tyler Durden, but not everyone is on the radar. She could have been homeless, maybe in the care system in her youth and then ejected with no support, ending up on the streets. If you're homeless, people walk past you, make no eye contact, it therefore makes sense that nobody would recognise the picture. And the homeless community aren't online to see it circulating. They are also probably well used to people just quietly dropping away so wouldn't report anything. Fair point but the lack of clothes, either on her or found nearby, that is too weird to ignore. What would a naked homeless person be doing in a place that requires a drive to get to, and then a walk through fields on top of the drive? Alright then, an immigrant maybe? Well, why would an immigrant be naked either? Forget the 'naked' for the moment, just think of types of people who would go missing and not be noticed, someone new to this country and on their own. Maybe, but your family back home would probably be looking for you by now, no replies to emails, no Facebook updates, it's been a year. And just because you're an immigrant doesn't mean nobody here knows you; you build a life here, make friends, get a job. Not always. Some people get smuggled here and don't get to build a life. Their job, home and peers are tied into their enslave-ment. Oh yeah, that makes sense. Wow, something we can finally agree on. It would also explain no boss or landlord piping up about a missing employee or tenant. The boss or landlord being the gang master who certainly doesn't want scrutiny. Or who perhaps even killed her. Maybe she tried to leave, or broke the rules. And any friends she had would be her fellow captives so they would be unable to come forward.

Ok, this is getting outlandish now, go to sleep. Or no, wake up, or not. It also explains being naked in the middle of nowhere, which until now has been the bizarre sticking point. Major hallmark of a dumped body. I would then shrug off this crime thriller I was writing in my feverish head, return to the more banal beginnings of my thought cycle and repeat the process again, and again, to this very day.

The first and only official thing I did was to book the funeral. I opted for burial in case her body should ever need to be exhumed for further investigation, or moved should family emerge, either to another grave in the UK, or even another country. I had also heard a radio show around that time where someone was trying to trace the grave of their infant brother, only to learn that he had been cremated and scattered. They had nowhere solid to focus their grief and were left feeling even more lost than they were at the start of their journey.

Lisa handed me the papers to sign and seeing the word 'unknown' where the deceased's name usually went hit me in the guts and lit a fire under me. I decided to use the space left by the gaping activity vacuum in this case to try and find her people, let them know where she was. She deserved the same efforts I made for everyone, even if I had no information to work with, that could be no excuse.

So I took to Twitter and asked the world: 'Does anyone out there know this woman?' I was met with hundreds of shares and replies. My mentions were filled with the picture preview from the news story and scrolling down them, as I constantly did, I saw nothing but her face, burning it even further into my retinas. Despite all of the noise though, no information came back. Hardly a surprise if after a year of appeals the police had received nothing either. What I did gain though was a lot of interest in and compassion for her. The visceral idea of dying alone, in fear, or sadness, or violence, and to be buried with no name, it affected people on a very primal level.

Everything we do in life, from our careers, building homes, practising hobbies, polishing skills, to having kids, it's all about legacy. We want to attain something and leave our mark, our basic fear is that we simply don't, that we fall short, are boxed in by money and circumstance and never try for that ambition or dream, but this was so much worse; to have the record erased completely as she had, it played into people's deepest darkest fears for themselves. In this way, death is very unifying. We are all going to die and we all fear it being a lonely, unremarked-upon ending, so we flock to those who have suffered that fate, treat them like death royalty, build tombs to unknown soldiers. Thus ironically ensuring that there is no such thing as a lonely death in this world. In fact, the lonelier the more universal. As the messages flooded in, it began to dawn on me that, ironically, her lonely story could perhaps be used to propel her back from the anonymous abyss. So I set about gaining permission from the press office to publicise her funeral date and ask for attendees. If I didn't find her people, I would bring some of my own.

This was very much the Plan B though, bubbling away in the background. Plan A remained in the forefront of my mind at this point. Find her, find her people. Every night after a contrasting day of admin and listening to the finer details of petty neighbour disputes, I would do a 180-degree flip into a world of gravity and mystery, sitting up in bed into the early hours, diving down one internet rabbit hole or another. Reddit crime forums, missing person's cold cases, myriad Google searches as my head swam with ideas for things I could try next. If nobody recognised her face, and if she couldn't be matched to any missing person's reports, then maybe the necklace she was wearing could be the key.

One such night I searched 'jewellery expert' and found an international association. I sent the picture of the antique necklace she was wearing through their contact page and asked if any of their members could identify its provenance. The police expert had described it as baroque but could there be any more clues in it? I had a reply straight away from a man in Hatton Garden, asking for a picture of the maker's mark. The next morning I emailed the police who took it out of evidence and did a close-up shot which I sent off. French, came the reply, or Swiss. French made some sense. She could have fallen off or jumped from a cross-channel boat, or floated across the water having died on their coastline. I then found myself sitting up at midnight trying to figure out how long a tide would take to bring a body from one side of the channel to the other. Losing sleep I could ill afford to on chasing shadows.

You see, on top of my usual pain and fatigue, I was a week into a virus that I had come down with the same morning the case arrived. It felt symbolic, staggering home half an hour after looking into her eyes, weak and giddy.

Unable to do much in the way of work, I had bridged the

gap by conducting those first Twitter enquiries from my sick bed that day, laying there until the room slowly turned pitch black, with only the glow of my laptop left. It was the one and only day of the case that I took off sick, the adrenaline of wanting to get to the bottom of things driving me back on, but I was running on fumes and so spent the whole time in a sickly fugue state, which only served to amplify the surreal nature of it all. Her face would appear whenever I closed my eyes to go to sleep. My feverish night sweats were accompanied by strange dreams in which she often appeared. Whilst half-dreaming and half-waking I would try to speak to her, get a name, an explanation. The blurring of realities meant that each time I slowly came out of my dream and back to full consciousness, I assigned shadows a human form and would have to switch a light on to dissipate them and assure myself it wasn't her at the foot of my bed. I would then dose up and limp back into work, pushing through the bin dramas and premises licence variations so I could get back to her.

The possible French connection set me off in another direction, and during one of my late nights I found an interview with someone who had started a missing person's charity for reasons which gave me pause. In France, after the age of 18, you have the right to disappear. Accordingly, adult disappearances don't always get followed up. The person who had started the charity was missing a family member and had created a website where they now compiled other people's un-investigated missing person's reports along with their own.

Perhaps this was why nobody matching my lady's description was found in the wider European missing person's database. If she was French, she might not even be on there. I knew that I may have been barking up the wrong tree, she might have bought a French necklace at an East End market, but in the absence of any other trees to bark up, I dusted off my GCSE Francais and composed an email to the charity founder, asking if she could translate the missing person's report and feature it on her site. Even if my lady was not French, the story would at least be on the mainland and in another language which would open her up to a wider audience.

Weeks passed and as with every avenue I tried, this too led to nothing. It was as though she had never existed in this world. As I visited with a friend one weekend and pushed her daughter along in the pram, I looked down and as was becoming usual at the time, my mind kept returning me to thoughts of my lady. She would have been safely in a pram once, happily chewing a cuddly toy. She would have gone to school, opened Christmas presents, laughed, grocery shopped, cried, done laundry, fallen in love, watched telly, everything banal and sublime and in between. I couldn't picture any of it though.

One of the main problems we all have with death is the here one minute, gone the next thing. How can someone be with us, so full of life, opinions, jokes, achievements and then be completely absent, forever? It doesn't compute. Her case was so much worse though because she was as absent in life as in death. There was a blackness when I tried to imagine her living and breathing. Not helped by the fact that all I knew of her was the artist's impression, which was so silent and abstract. A sketch of an imaginary character. Not a real person. I wanted to bring her back, make her real again.

With only a couple of weeks left until the funeral, I was running out of time, and ideas. I had sent emails to every European foreign embassy in London asking them to put up her picture, in case she was an immigrant and her family came over looking for her. Then trafficking organisations asking for her picture to go up in shelters and rescue centres, in case that theory held any water and people who had crossed paths and escaped might recognise her. Then homeless and women's shelters in all of the surrounding towns. As time went on, my fingers hovered over the keyboard, a blank search box on the screen, not knowing what to type anymore. I was done.

Luckily I had gained some traction with the UK press. All of the local newspapers for the county took her story up, and gradually she popped up in local newspapers further along the coast, then inland and in the end, even as far as Scotland. Some national newspapers followed, along with the BBC. No information came from any of it though, which confirmed my theory that she probably wasn't from round these here parts, with my darker theory nagging away at the back of my mind. After emailing all European news agencies and getting no response, I finally had to admit defeat. I had done all I could with my limited reach. She was out there for all to see, and anyone who knew her and couldn't come forward for whatever reason would at least know where she was now, where she would be buried and when.

I then made an uneasy peace with it all and turned my full attention back to Plan B; not allowing her to leave this world alone for a second time. My Tweets and the subsequent press coverage had gained the promise of some attendees and a couple of floral tributes. The kindness of strangers got me thinking and I wondered if I could ask companies to help me with the types of things my budget couldn't cover, like posh funeral flowers. A cheeky ask but I didn't have anything else left to do on this case and they could only say no.

One lunchtime as the pub quiz questions were in full flow, I fired off emails at a selection of florists, expecting a rejection from each one, or at the very best the offer of maybe one small pity bunch. I got an emphatic yes from all but two of them and live-commentated on my successes to the room as they rolled in throughout the day. Got a bunch. Got another bunch. And another one. After a succession of bouquets I hit pay dirt, with one company replying to say that their entire office had been touched by the story and they were sending a hundred-quid coffin spray.

Flowers secured and emboldened by my success, I decided to go for an even cheekier ask: a gravestone. It was bad enough that she was being buried unknown, but without a memorial she would remain unidentifiable forever after.

As before, I turned lunch time into grift time and sent multiple emails to various masonry companies. I was expecting nothing this time. Flowers are one thing, a gravestone is quite another. I made the licensing officer behind me jump as I cheered at the almost immediate offer of a grave marker – one of those ground stakes with a little plaque – and I was in the middle of saying to them that this was as good as I could expect and actually they are quite nice, so that's fine, when I was suddenly offered two gravestones in quick succession. I never thought I would have to turn someone away. I kept the marker as it would be a useful temporary measure whilst the ground settled, and could remain at the opposite end of the grave to the stone when that arrived, and then took the first stone mason up on their offer; it was all coming together. But then the stone mason interrupted my giddy joy to warn me that there was usually a hefty fee to be paid to the cemetery to lay a stone, so before they started work, I needed to check this out. I couldn't pay out for anything beyond the funeral so, suitably deflated, I got on the phone to the graveyard to beg them to waive the fee. I expected a hard no and for my gravestone coup to fall at the first hurdle, but when I explained her story they said yes right away.

'People really feel for you,' I told her, as she wandered in and out of the phantasmagoria of my stage-one sleep that night. 'Whatever awful thing happened to you at the end, I hope you can feel all of this kindness wherever you are.'

She said nothing as usual. The closed mouth of the artist's impression clearly informed my subconscious mind's visualisations of her. Her half-smile always took the edge off though. She wasn't surly, just calmly and silently approving, from a realm where she no longer worried about the petty matter of what had become of her in life. That's how I like to think about death, not from the life side of it, where we fear the moment and the loss of ourselves, but from the other side, the nothing side, where we don't care, can't care, because we're not able to. For those who fear death I always say, did you mind that really long bit of nothing before you were born? If someone approached you whilst in that neutral state and told you they could give you life, make you corporeal, with just a few pesky downsides, like feeling pain, anxiety, unrequited love, being too cold, too hot, thirsty, itchy, needing to buy a new boiler every ten years, scrambling around for money to pay rent, you'd probably say, 'nah, I'm alright thanks'. Life is the hard bit, good, but still hard, death is the well-earned kip at the end.

I took the next couple of days off work to get my breath back, to get away from the run-of-the-mill tasks that felt increasingly unimportant for the moment and to go to the site of my dreams; the place of her death. Perhaps by scratching the itch it would stop them, maybe I would commune better with her there, or maybe it just had to be done for the sheer sake of filling the activity void around the case.

I arrived at the point where the road ended and the off-road dirt track began. The track wound upwards to the high ground above the sea and arrived in a small car park exposed to the winds that whipped up from the water and across the exposed open countryside. Struggling to open the car door without it shutting back on me, I eventually got out and took the hiking trail down the other side of the hill that led to the beach. The wind battered me, I could taste the salt air on my lips, feel it coating my hair until it was damp and stiff. The coastline slowly came into view along with a shock of white cliffs. I wondered if she had walked this very path before she died, likely, as it was one of very few access routes, and if so where she had come from before that, and before the before. I emerged onto the beach, crunching across the stones, as I made my way to the river cutting through it, out to sea. This was where she was found. I stood and listened to the waves roll in and out, over the stones, pulling them out and pushing them back in with that rhythmic rattle. I watched ramblers, dog walkers and an entire school trip stepping over the spot where her body once lay.

The wind was now howling and the waves were high, just like in my dreams. The loneliness of the scene wasn't diminished by all of the activity going on around and about it, if anything seeing life marching on at this spot made it all the more poignant. The song lyric, 'why does the sea rush to shore, don't they know it's the end of the world', came to life, and I thought about the person who was surely out there, missing her that deeply. I staggered back up the hill, legs burning, pain condition punishing me for the hiking I had just made us do, and retreated back inside the car. As the door slammed and cut the howling wind dead, there was silence. This, coupled with the view, an expanse of nothing, with a grey sky looming above it, filled me with the desolation and pain this place must have held for her at the end, whatever the nature of it. I sat there and just cried.

The following day I visited Martin at home to see how he was getting on with the hard task of eulogising someone about whom nothing was known. He talked through some of his ideas for readings and then we chatted about the case, the lady, our feelings about it all. In his job he handled many difficult assignments; suicides, kids, men his age, with children of his own children's age, having to be lifted up to place flowers on the coffin. He had to meet the families in the raw first stages of their grief to gather the information needed to pull together a service, usually ending up indirectly in the role of a counsellor. He had to connect enough to do his job well but keep a professional distance so as to avoid getting sucked into the emotion of the day, for which he was meant to be the professional glue holding everything together. This need for a difficult-to-achieve balance, feeling it all but at a remove, struck a chord with me. He was making a really good and quite deep point about how to do this when his dog suddenly picked up and started continuously biting down on a squeaky rubber chicken. It broke the sombre mood and served as a much needed reminder that life is light and shade. It also got us back down to business.

For the service, we had decided not to book the chapel. The usual file in, stand, be seated, would be followed by, what? It would just underline her status as an unclaimed unknown. No name to utter, no stories to tell, no eulogy, no meaningful readings or favourite music to play us in and then out again. Better to focus on the pageantry and ritual. We decided to follow her coffin to the grave, then he would do a reading or two, say the words of committal, we could scatter flowers and soil and then place the grave marker.

When I returned to my desk the next day, I had an email from a member of the public who wanted to host a wake. I welled up at this kind offering of yet another traditional funeral element that the lady, due to lack of loved ones, would otherwise be denied. I was reading the email as I simultaneously listened to a voicemail from Lisa. Someone had contacted them, asking for my details as they wanted to host a wake. I called straight back and said not to worry, so and so had reached me by email.

'Wait,' she said. 'That's not the person who called us.'

Yes reader, my lady had two people wanting to throw her a wake. For the entirety of the case I had resisted using a nickname for her. Lisa called her Jackie and Steve called her Olga. I hesitated because ultimately I wanted to find out her real name, but 'two wakes' was too hard to resist. ''Ere she comes, old two wakes, with her two wakes.' I replied to the first person's email explaining the situation and asking for permission to pass their details to the other would-be organiser. Consent duly gained, they went off together and booked a pub in the town where the funeral was to be held.

And I went off to carry out my final task in the dying hours before the funeral. That evening I went to a supermarket to collect a bunch of flowers they had donated. The cashier read the email from her store manager on my phone and, recognising the case we were messaging about from the news coverage, threw in a second bunch on top. As I turned away from the tills to walk back out I was faced with a rack of local newspapers, and in a scene fit for a gritty TV drama, her face was on every front page, staring curiously out at me to see what flowers I had managed to blag for her. 'You haunting me during the day now too?' I thought and possibly mouthed, or even muttered.

And so, after a month that had been both the longest and the quickest, the busiest and the most stagnant, the bleakest and the brightest, the day finally came around. After everything, all of the energy and ceaseless activity, I was still where

I had been on day one; nowhere. I would be burying her nameless with nobody who loved her present. Ever the pig-headed trier, I woke up early to speak to the local BBC radio news, air her story one more time, get the word out, invite all -comers, hoping for that call saying 'hold the funeral, we've found the family', then I stuck my supermarket-freebie flowers in a bucket of water and shoved them into the footwell of my car before setting off.

I went via the station to pick up a mate who had come all the way from London for the funeral. None other than the celebrity cat-sitter, Al. In his own words, he came to support his friend, he came to try and lay some of his own stuff to rest, he came because he's a writer; he didn't know why he came. And his experience was by no means unique.

We stood in the cemetery car park as it filled up, me, Al, Martin, Steve, and a lovely BBC producer called Mary who was recording the audio of the day – she had come with me to Martin's and his dog had fallen in love with her boom coat, whose fur resembled his own – and in the buzz of conver-sation you could pick out words; sad, suicidal, depression, lonely. Then as the gates had to be shut and cars turned away, I realised how much she had chimed with people who felt alone and adrift. Lost souls reaching out to a lost soul. They came for themselves as much as her. They came in place of loved ones. They came as loved ones. They came 115 strong.

When the hearse pulled up at the cemetery gates, I realised that I would finally, after weeks of hallucinatory chats, be united with her in person. I went numb and found myself rooted to the ground. The gate was opened for her and the car turned the corner, pulling up right alongside me. The buzz of conversation faded and everyone fell silent. As I realised that I couldn't actually see her coffin for flowers, the numbness, clearly a temporary short circuit after weeks of intense feelings, gave way. They were happy tears though. Relief that, despite not finding out who she was, I had packed out her funeral and showered her in flowers and love.

Jodie got out and walked around to the front of the car, getting ready to lead the procession. With absolutely no verbal direction, the crowd, wordlessly and as one, followed her and the hearse down the winding cemetery path. I followed behind, now also joined by my mum who had decided to come along. She had brought a packed lunch for me including a full packet of Party Rings. This was the second funeral she had brought Party Rings to, I might add, the first one being her best friend's. Possibly the most inappropriate of all the snacks for a funeral but delicious so I'll allow it.

As we turned a bend and the path dipped down I gasped as I saw the full extent of the cortège. Two hundred metres or more, with her at the head of them. This anonymous person who could so easily have been forgotten and lost, the focal point of everything. As we all gradually arrived at the spot, flowers piled up beside the open grave as people who had brought their own added to the ones from inside the hearse. Jodie and the bearers – surely her band name in waiting – turned crowd controllers as they manoeuvred the mourners from the path to the grass and into a semi-circular formation before resuming their zen-like poise and walking the coffin over to the grave edge.

It was a beautiful, sunny, windless day, with just the sound of birdsong for Martin to compete with. Everyone in place, he began. Instead of the usual eulogy, he acknowledged that nothing was known of this woman and that in lieu of the family or friends who would otherwise mourn her, it fell to us to pay our respects and bid farewell to her. He spoke about death and he spoke about life. His readings covering both subjects; Van Dyke's 'Gone from my Sight' and WH Davies' 'Leisure' respectively. The former poem depicting death as someone disappearing from view but not really being gone, rather elsewhere, whether you interpret that as an afterlife or living on in memories. The latter reminding those still present to live fully and take stock; 'a poor life this, if full of care, we have no time to stop and stare'. Then followed the final words of committal, spoken as she was lowered into the ground.

The main service concluded, the floor was opened up for members of the public to speak, and many did. Poems were read, self-penned eulogies given, reflections made. Thoughts on what her life might have been like, how society looks the other way as people fall through the cracks, hope expressed that she didn't suffer and had managed some happiness before her life was cut short. This wasn't just her funeral, it felt like a lament for anyone who had been lost or forgotten, and a promise to do better by each other. And then, finally, as nobody else stepped forward, people began to gradually drift off.

When everyone had dispersed, I went to the graveside and looked down at her coffin. I wanted to stand with her for a moment, take it all in, and then try to declare it over and done with. I had a genuine concern that I was going to turn into one of those retired cop parodies, never dropping that last unsolved case. I didn't know what to say to her, too much had happened, too much to say oftentimes brings you full circle to nothing, so I stood there silently knowing that she would know what I was thinking before whispering goodbye and walking away. As I left, the BBC asked me for an interview and in front of her open grave I, shell-shocked and looking worse for wear, as I later found out on catch-up TV, managed to articulate some brief thoughts on what had just happened.

'She's nobody's, so she's everybody's; she's all of us.'

When one of the other journalists present produced a national newspaper story days later crediting the funeral as the work of the local community – I won't mention the publication but to say that their level of research in this case, not speaking to me, Martin or the funeral director on the day, explains a lot about their paper's usual output – I took great pains to correct it. The amendments were made and their heart-warming yarn was replaced with the much more heart-warming truth of the council safety net. Far less romantic than local people banding together to bury a lost soul, but actually, this wouldn't be as nice as it sounded. The local community doesn't have the time, resources and emotional bandwidth to bury and cremate every person in the area with nobody to do it for them. Nor would all cases appeal to their hearts and imaginations. Her anonymity, tragedy and mystery had been her great draw. Old Jean or Dodgy Matthew wouldn't have had the same cachet. The council helps all, whoever you are, that's the real story that needed to be heard.

I looked back over my shoulder one last time, at the open grave, the cubic tonne of flowers, and then chased up the path to join the others on the walk back to the car park. My mum headed off, packed lunch and Party Rings still intact, with all the emotion of the day I simply had no stomach, which says a lot as I never turn them down.

Steve, having just got back from leave, had to head off too, back to the office to catch up with himself. Knowing that I would have been entirely unable to concentrate on work had I returned to the office, I had taken the afternoon off in anticipation, and also to attend the super combo wake because how could I not? Martin, Mary and Al joined me and we drove into town, parking in a local supermarket behind the street the pub was on. As we walked through the car park, a woman who had been at the service appeared out of nowhere. She wanted to tell Martin what a beautiful ceremony it had been. Then before we knew it she was sobbing and holding onto him as she explained that she had gone to those same cliffs to take her own life a year before. Then weeks earlier she had tried to end her life again, but had spat the pills out at the last minute. An estranged friend had spotted the funeral story in the local paper and contacted her about it. They had agreed to forgive one another and go.

This theme continued when we arrived at the pub. Everyone we spoke to mentioned depression, loneliness, anxiety, suicide attempts. Her death had not been ruled a suicide but neither had it not been and all of the mystery surrounding it allowed people to project onto her whatever issues they were grappling with themselves. They ended up sitting together in a roped-off area of the pub, eating buffet food and bonding all afternoon. People walked away from that day knowing they weren't the only one, feeling less alone, and due to the friendships made, actually being less alone. She would never know it, but through her death, the lady had helped dozens of people, perhaps saved some.

And with that, it was all over. Physically and emotionally drained, Al and I headed back to my house in a kind of shock to attempt a normal and much-needed thing; dinner. Aside from the wake snacks we hadn't eaten all day and, wandering around in the ephemeral haze of it all, hadn't really had the time or inclination to notice. But now it hit us like a truck and vast amounts of takeaway food were ordered as we tried to eat ourselves back to reality whilst the day's events played out on the local BBC evening news in the form of flickering lights and faint words, some my own, floating through from the dusky darkness of the next room where the telly was playing to itself. We talked about everything, processing what we had seen, what it had meant to everyone there that day from individuals to the news journalists.

Weeks of chasing her ghost had come to nothing but, at the same time, everything. The blank slate of her story allowed myriad people to transpose their own, and the media to transpose all of ours. Realisations were made, friendships, kind gestures. She was bigger than whoever she had once been and just as each of my cases became part of me, she became part of the lived experience of everyone there that day and everyone watching that night. Her lost story became a hundred other stories. I like to tell myself that anyway.

As night fell, it was time for Al to hop a train back to the Big Smoke. After such an emotional day it felt like a wrench, leaving each other, leaving her, but the saving mundane grace of work in the morning helped to forcibly break the spell and we quietly set off for the station. As we turned the corner out of my road, the moon was looming above us at twice its normal size, so bright that everything in the empty streets – trees, cars, pavement – had an other-worldly silver sheen to them. The train was in twenty minutes, but the sky was calling, so I darted us through the back streets and got us to the beach for an unobstructed and grander view. As we pulled up on the empty front, the sea was illuminated bright white, a giant shard of silver light flowed towards us from the moon like a prison search lamp; an uninterrupted beam from the horizon all the way to the shore edge.

We got out of the car and, too impatient to get to the next set of steps, jumped through the metal fence along the promenade down onto the pebble beach, the stones clacking as we landed. We ran towards the shore laughing, shouting, swearing, and pointing at the sky, as we stumbled over the stones, which slipped from under us and sank beneath us, making running near impossible, but ran we somehow did. Then, panting for breath, we reached the water's edge and as our breathing slowly settled we stood there and just stared up at it, mesmerised.

'It's her,' he said, breaking the silence. 'It's her. She's saying thank you.'

Now as you know, I don't believe in that kind of thing. But it's a nice place to end.

Postlude

I went back to her grave six months after the funeral. More than a year since her body had been found. I still didn't know her name.

I was there to watch the laying of her gravestone… Ah yes, hi, here we are, back at the beginning, well, the end. One and the same really, as with the circle of life.

I had arrived early, before the groundskeeper or the cemetery manager. The stone had been brought down the night before and placed on a bench near her grave. 'To the unknown lady', it read, and gave the date and location of her discovery.

The grave was not bare though. A wilted bunch of flowers and a brown Christmas wreath were laid out, along with her temporary marker. The flowers had been placed there by the guardian of her grave, a lady who attended the funeral and did one of the most moving of the public readings that day. She was shy and unassuming, but her self-penned eulogy, though spoken softly, had searing impact. She had resolved to look after the lady, whom she named Grace, until her family found her, attending her grave weekly with new flowers, removing leaves, and gradually adding items to it; eventually a fence, a rose bush and a large angel statue.

She arrived early too and was starting to tell me something when the cemetery staff came into view at the end of the path. We agreed to pick it up afterwards and greeted what turned out to be the groundskeeper, cemetery manager and the whole local town council who had come down for what was to be a mini service. The stone was placed, a few words were said and we stood silently for a while before everyone dispersed, leaving us free to continue our conversation.

Before we did, the old flowers needed removing and the bunches we had each bought for the occasion needed to be cut and arranged in the grave vases the guardian had bought. As we were doing this, a people carrier pulled up and four women got out and set up garden chairs around a grave just along the way that was absolutely heaving with flowers and balloons. From the floral rendition of a Calor Gas can, I surmised they were travellers. They turned on the car stereo and blasted out Dolly Parton's greatest hits as they stood around the grave hugging and crying. It was the strangest and the best kind of mourning I had ever seen.

About halfway through the third song, '9 to 5' as I recall, they clocked us and wandered over.

'Does anyone know who she is yet?' One woman asked.

'You know about the case?' I asked back, in surprise. She did. Her mother, who was in the grave four doors down had attended the funeral just months before. We told them that she remained unknown but that it was nice that she had a friendly neighbour now. As Dolly Parton continued to fill the graveyard they hugged us both, cried, talked about traveller funeral traditions and told us about their mum and her love for the country and western legend. As they drifted back over to her grave, we quietly bopped away to their soundtrack as we cleared leaves and dead flowers. Another of the many surreal moments this job has provided me with.

I picked up the wreath and said, 'Nice idea, getting her a Christmas present.'

Grave guardian paused and said, 'That wasn't me, it's actually what I wanted to talk to you about.'

She then went to her car to get something that had been placed inside it. I won't say what she brought back, in case it gets anyone in bother, but the item had a very specific origin and significance. A significance that matched my theory. It could have just been a random well-wisher, one of the many people who knew her story, but surely they would just opt for a generic bunch of flowers. It seemed more likely that it was someone who knew her origins, who perhaps shared her origins; who knew her. If this was the case, I no longer needed to worry about finding her, as I had continued to try to do for some time after the funeral, because someone out there already knew who she really was and that was enough. It would have to be.

So, as I rhetorically asked at the start, how did I end up at the graveside of an unclaimed body, having a chat with the wind and the soil on my day off?

Well, now you know.

Did I ever find the balance? Well, I'm still doing house searches and attending funerals on my days off, still picking up calls on evenings and weekends, fielding messages in my personal DMs, popping to the bank with an invoice during my own shopping errands, driving ashes about the place. So, in short, no, not really. But I don't think I want to entirely. The second I draw a line between myself and the job, I deem my people to be a task and place them and their family on a par with a website update or licence variation. If you're going to do a job so tied up in life, you have to let it into your own and draw on that. The love you have for your own friends and family, what you would want for them, projecting that back onto your actions in each case.

In terms of my confidence and authority, I have gone from faking it to making it thanks to my people and the knowledge I have gained through them. From helping to edit Steve's guidance to rewriting it from scratch according to my own experiences, adding in all the new variables that arise along the way, curating all the shortcuts, hacks and tips. I can wrap up a life by lunchtime now, an improvement on the six hours I spent on Carl's admin, digging through papers and then searching for who to call. I know the numbers to dial now, who to ask for, what they will want to know. I have cover letters ready to send to bank bereavement teams who, despite these types of funerals being reasonably frequent, usually act like they've never heard of such a thing before. Some of them are pretty good, but more often than not it's like Groundhog Day. I'm Bill Murray, speaking French, playing piano, making ice sculptures and they're Ned saying 'Phil?' as though for the first time.

My website pages have been judged to be of the top

standard by a funeral poverty charity, turning up in the slides of a training event I went to to show councils how it should be done. I have trained up two more people since Steve moved teams which will allow me to let go a little on my days off and, along with my written guidance, will ensure that if I get hit by a bus the department can carry on uninterrupted. Because, as I replied to a colleague who recently said, 'What would this place do without you?' – replace me, like I'd never existed. Remember that we disappear, life goes on. It shouldn't stop you from giving your all while you're here, but if you're stressed at your desk, remember some day there will be someone else sitting there in your place; we're all temps in a way.

The technical stuff and the practical balance was never really the big problem though, that's all just a matter of time and logistics. What of the emotional balancing act? Well, progress has been made, of sorts. In part because my health demands it. The emotional strain takes a physical toll and when you have pain that is brought on by exertion and stress you have to practice self-care.

Getting used to things has helped. No life is the same and every case is different, but experience builds resilience. I well up nowadays rather than cry or bawl; feel it but move on. Like the morbid Mary Poppins I mentioned earlier, who cares about those kids dearly for the duration of the job but has to emotionlessly fly away when she's finished. As with the practical balance, I have to remain open, but for the good of my sanity, not all the way open. Recent moments which would have floored me early on; learning during a service that the closing song was the same one played at the funeral of the deceased's own son, seeing a bottle opener on the keys of the alcoholic who killed himself with booze and pills, glimpsing a note on a kitchen cork board which said 'I'm right here, love you' from the wife who died nine years before the deceased and who, from the foliage completely covering his bedroom window and the funeral order of service on the bedside table, very obviously never got over it. Nowadays I feel that slight gut punch, feel privileged to have been party to it, breathe deep, then back in the room.

When it comes to my physical nerves and stomach, I can still get spooked or be made to jump upon entering properties, just as I did at Robert's house on day one. Like the false leg of a chap whose body had been removed without it, left leaning against the armchair where he died and sitting at such a jaunty 'I've been expecting you' angle that it made me scream as I came up the stairs. The black handbag of a woman who was being looked into as a possible suicide, placed deliberately in the middle of a perfectly-made chintzy floral bed. Everything in the room light pastel, frilly and lacy and then the ominous black bag sitting there seeming to say, 'Look inside, there's a message from the deceased'.

I knew what it was before I opened it. All of her papers and ID for me or whoever to find. She had already got rid of most of her clothes and nearly all the downstairs furniture. I walked through empty rooms with just impression marks in the carpet, the outline of her life. She did the house clearance so we didn't have to, erasing her home before possibly erasing herself. These eerie moments, as usual, were offset by something that reconnected you to the living world as we then found she had a cupboard full of hoarded Covid-times toilet roll and had also stolen the bins of everyone in the street. A neighbour knocked during the search who was convinced she was the phantom bin thief. She was unmasked as such that day as we opened the side gate and found all seven in a row.

Physically, I'm better at dealing with the blood, maggots, flies, dirt, but never entirely immune. Opening a freezer which had been turned off at the wall weeks earlier to find it full to the brim of rotting meat, blood dripping out like the lift scene from The Shining and a smell so bad it made Steve, an experienced officer, have to leave the house. I only stayed, eyes watering, gagging, because I knew if I walked away I would have a hard time going back. When he returned with the wheelie bin I pulled the contents out, hot to the touch, the motion of maggots tangible, blood slopping all over the place. You can never get used to that, nor should you, that would be odd. But you deal with it and don't baulk or complain. At least you're alive to be taking the bin out.

And life, it continues to get richer too, with each case. I get Tweeted videos of Adam's train sets by the club, messaged by Donald's ex-partner to update me on the family successfully rebuilding, invited to the scattering of ashes, and even today I got a WhatsApp months after a funeral from a relative who wanted to say she that hadn't forgotten my kindness. I'm kept up to date on all of these lives that go on after the deaths that ushered them into my orbit. Because it's life that is really at the heart of all these stories.

Whether it's in the rediscovery or the closing of the book, death has the power to underscore our stories one last time, or even change the story going forward. And I am honoured to be there to see it up close and take the lessons into my own life, which is set happily beside the seaside per my childhood bucket list.

The amount of funerals I have attended since starting this job would usually mark me out as someone experiencing a horrific run of personal luck or as a gloating serial killer, but I am just a council worker, charged with Section 46 funerals and I am here along with many like me if you should ever need us. Here also to tell you that it's not how you die, the opulence of your send-off, the amount of flowers. Your funeral isn't a scorecard. You lived a life, whether anyone remembers it or not, but we will do our best to find it. Just meet us halfway and leave some clues though, please.

And with that, we reach our not-so-neat conclusion and just draw an arbitrary finish line, because it's not over. I mean, where do you stop a book about unstoppable death? I'll be working on another case as you read this. They just keep coming. Until one day it'll be you, and me, and everyone we ever knew.

So I suppose the neat conclusion would be to keep that in mind, befriend death, turn a light on, extinguish those shadows, and live well; because that's the bit that matters.